MORE
SENIOR
MOMENTS

MORE SENIOR MOMENTS

(THE ONES WE FORGOT)

Shelley Klein

Michael O'Mara Books Limited

First published in Great Britain in 2007 by
Michael O'Mara Books Limited
9 Lion Yard
Tremadoc Road
London SW4 7NQ

A CIP catalogue record for this book is available from the British Library

ISBN: 978-1-84317-256-7

1 3 5 7 9 10 8 6 4 2

www.mombooks.com

Designed and typeset by Design 23

Printed and bound in Great Britain by Clays Ltd, St Ives plc

INTRODUCTION

Senior moments – those disastrous episodes of lunacy when common sense vanishes, your memory deserts you and you can't remember your own name or what day of the week it is – come in all shapes and sizes, and alarmingly can strike at any age. Of course, you might put the phenomenon down to the stress of modern-day life and the fact that we are now having to cope with careers as well as bringing up a family, shopping in super-size retail parks, entertaining friends and relatives, arranging foreign holidays and throwing dinner parties, but this isn't the case at all. Senior moments have plagued man for centuries; we can trace the trend as far back as the sixteenth century, and there are certainly examples of them having occurred well before this date too, only I can't seem to find the piece of paper I noted them down on.

Just as senior moments are not confined to a specific age group, neither are they any respecters of class or intelligence. The world-renowned scientist Albert Einstein not only lost his wife, but he also succeeded in mislaying a cheque for $1,500, which had been awarded to him by the Rockefeller Foundation. For months, Einstein had used the slip of paper as a bookmark, then misplaced the book itself. Accountants at the Foundation, realizing that he hadn't banked the first cheque, cancelled it and wrote another one out to him. Einstein, meanwhile, having forgotten all about the first cheque, wrote back confusedly, 'What is this for?'

Even prime ministers and presidents are not exempt from having the odd senior moment. George W. Bush is renowned for his terrible way with words and Ronald Reagan was always making dreadful bloopers – frequently forgetting the name of the country he was visiting. Another US president who seemed to have problems remembering things was Dwight D. Eisenhower who, in 1953, created a new government department called Health, Education and Welfare – otherwise known as HEW. Eisenhower, however, could never remember the full meaning of the abbreviation and was often heard referring to the department as that of Health, Welfare and Whatnot.

Among the many professions that figure in this collection are doctors, dentists, vets, lawyers and teachers, but perhaps the stupidest people – the people for whom one should really feel most pity – are the apparently large number of thieves, robbers and general law-breakers out there who fail to use the brains they were born with. Imagine falling asleep in the middle of a shop you've just robbed . . . or leaving your CV behind in a bank you have just held up at gunpoint? There is little hope for characters such as these and jail is obviously the best place for them.

Although senior moments can occur at any age, it is during the decline of life – when you're losing your hair, your teeth and your eyesight whilst putting on weight and discovering you've acquired a nice collection of varicose veins – that they start happening frequently. The cause of senior moments can boil down to physical health or rather a lack of it, hence a large number of anecdotes in this volume concern not only the medical profession, but also, sadly, funeral parlours and cemeteries. Of course, dying and death are not laughing matters, yet who cannot laugh at the one about the man who suffered a heart attack while fetching a cabbage from his vegetable patch? 'Oh my God, that must have been terrible!' exclaimed a neighbour to the dead man's wife.

'Yes, it was,' the wife replied.

'So what did you do?'

'Opened a can of peas instead.'

Indeed, if you are going to suffer the indignity of a senior moment, one sure-fire way to cover up your embarrassment is to use humour.

There are numerous coping strategies when it comes to preventing your nearest and dearest from dragging you off to the local lunatic asylum. Perhaps the best method of all is to create a diversion. Forgotten where you put the car keys? Scream suddenly and point through the window to a distant spot at the bottom of your garden or street. Tell your spouse/daughter/son-in-law that they must investigate what is going on as a matter of urgency. Tell them that you can smell smoke/see flames/hear screams/any other suitably melodramatic occurrences. Once they have left the premises, you are free to search the house in peace, without the horror of people mocking you. If, however, creating a diversion doesn't work, lying is a perfectly honourable alternative. You've lost your glasses and some bright spark points out that you are wearing them on top of your head? Tell them that you weren't in fact looking for those glasses; you were searching for your *reading glasses*, your *sunglasses*, glasses into which to pour orange juice, but do not, on any account, resort to divulging the bitter truth.

If all of the above fail miserably, you can always take refuge in the fact that – like Sigourney Weaver in *Alien* – 'you are not alone'. Thousands of people suffer from senior momentitus every year and most, if not all of them, live to see another day. Hopefully none of us will repeat these experiences, but what is absolutely without doubt is that we will all grow older and fatter at some point and, although dieting might see to the spare tyre around your waist, and a visit to the plastic surgeon might remedy laughter lines, sagging breasts and drooping eyelids, what cannot so easily be put right is the fact that we all do inane things. The only real hope any of us have is that, through reading a book such as this, and laughing at other people's mistakes, we can find comfort in numbers because, from vicar to viceroy and from poet laureate to Oscar-nominated actor, we've all fallen victim to the curse of senior momentitus . . .

SHELLEY KLEIN, 2007

OH, BABY!

We have all stood in front of the X-ray machine at the airport, uncertain which of our possessions to offer up. Do I hand over my computer? Will the X-rays affect my digital camera? In December 2006, at Los Angeles International Airport, a fifty-six-year-old grandmother was obviously suffering from a senior moment when she decided to place her one-month-old grandchild in the monitoring tray and push the infant through the machine. Security staff were horrified when they caught sight of the baby's outline on their computers, quickly pulling the child out. No harm was done, except perhaps to the grandmother's pride.

HAT'S YOUR LOT

It is a little-known fact that the eighteenth-century author Edward Gibbon, famed for writing *The Decline and Fall of the Roman Empire*, hated doing any exercise. On one occasion, having stayed at his good friend Lord Sheffield's country estate for several weeks, Gibbon decided that it was time to leave and return back to his own house. However, Gibbon couldn't find his hat. He looked high and low for it, eventually discovering that the hat was sitting in the hall where it had been ever since his arrival. Gibbon had forgotten to leave the house during his entire stay.

HUNGER STRIKES

An elderly couple are sitting watching television when the old man decides that he is hungry for some ice cream.

'Darling, I'm going to head to the kitchen and get myself a dish of ice cream. Do you want some, too?'

'Yes please, sweetheart, sounds good. But you better write down what you're going out there for or else you'll forget,' replies his wife.

'I will not!' retorts the old man. 'In fact, tell me what you want on it and I'll remember that, too.'

'OK,' says the old lady, 'I'll have chocolate sauce on mine. But I'm willing to bet you will forget.'

The old man heads out to the kitchen and disappears for about twenty or thirty minutes. Finally he emerges, carrying a plate of scrambled eggs.

'See, I told you you'd forget!' exclaims the old woman triumphantly.

'What do you mean? What did I forget?' demands her husband.

'You fool,' says the old dear. 'You forgot my bacon!'

SENIOR PRAYER

Grant me the senility to forget the people I never liked anyway, the good fortune to run into the ones I do and the eyesight to tell the difference, amen.

FLUCK IT!

Not a lot of people know that the English film actress Diana Dors was actually called Diana Fluck. When the blonde bombshell was asked by her hometown to open their annual fête, the local vicar was called upon to introduce her to the crowd by her real name. Naturally, the vicar was somewhat nervous as the big day approached, and his nerves grew and grew until finally the moment was upon him. According to local legend, the vicar concluded his introductory speech with the words, 'And now, here she is, the woman the whole world knows as "Diana Dors", but whom we will always remember as our own Diana Clunt . . . '

STAGE PRESENCE

The internationally famous film actor Dustin Hoffman is perhaps best known for his roles in *The Graduate* and *Midnight Cowboy*, but he once took to the stage in Arthur Miller's *Death of a Salesman*, in which he played the part of Willy Loman. Frank Rich, theatre critic for *The New York Times*, must surely have been suffering a chronic senior moment when he wrote in a review: 'I was overwhelmed by the tragic smallness of Dustin Hoffman's Willy.'

'Age doesn't matter, unless you're a cheese.'
– BILLIE BURKE, ACTRESS

WHAT'S IN A NAME?

An elderly gentleman was invited round to the house of an old married couple he was friendly with for dinner one evening. He was impressed by the way that the husband called his wife by many endearing nicknames: 'honey', 'sweetheart', 'petal', 'love', 'precious', 'darling', among many others. The couple had been married for over fifty years, but were clearly still very much in love. When the wife was in the kitchen, the man leaned over and said to his host, 'I must say, I think it's wonderful that, after all these years, you still call your wife by these loving names.' His host sighed. 'I have to tell you the truth,' he said. 'I forgot her name about ten years ago.'

SPEECH THERAPY

The following is an example of how a senior moment can affect the high and mighty just as easily as common folk.

One day, George Salmon, a nineteenth-century Regius Professor of Divinity at Trinity College, Dublin, brought with him to church a sermon that he had already preached to his congregation the year before. Undaunted by this oversight (or just too ashamed to admit that his memory wasn't as good as it once was), he is said to have explained the repetition away by reasoning that at least half the congregation was probably not present when he had first preached the sermon, and that therefore the words would be brand new to them; that a quarter of the congregation, despite having heard it before, would probably not mind hearing it a second time; and that the final quarter of the congregation who had heard it the first time, would no doubt not remember they had and therefore, like the first quarter, would not mind hearing it again.

Now that's how to dig yourself out of a mess!

UNIVERSITY CHALLENGED

The annual Oxford/Cambridge Boat Race is one of the most famous sporting events in the world. Commentating on the event in 1949, John Snagge uttered the immortal words: 'I don't know who's ahead – it's either Oxford or Cambridge.'

TILL MEMORY LOSS DO US PART

Blonde movie star Doris Day was walking in Beverly Hills one day when she was stopped by a man. Thinking that he was a fan, Day greeted him politely and continued on her way.

'Don't you remember me?' the man shouted after her.

'No,' the actress replied. 'Should I?'

'Well, you didn't have that many husbands,' retorted her second husband, saxophonist George Weidler.

BURNT OFFERINGS

The author James Joyce grew so blind in his old age that his handwriting became almost illegible. In the *Ulysses* manuscript, the Circe episode was so undecipherable that the husband of Joyce's typist mistook the pages for scrap paper and threw them into the fire. Not a very happy day for English literature . . .

DOGGY ESCALATORS

One day, Melanie Warner, who lives in Brighton with her husband and two children, decided to take her elderly, rather cantankerous grandmother on a shopping trip to London. Her grandmother, who in her youth had worked for a local newspaper checking grammar and spelling for the reporters, had been feeling a little depressed of late owing to her increasing years. A shopping trip would be just the ticket . . . or so Melanie thought. They caught the train into the centre of London, with Melanie deciding that the best way to get to Oxford Street was to take the Underground. Marshalling her grandmother through the ticket hall, Melanie was approaching the escalators with her grandmother in tow, when suddenly the old woman came to a halt.

'What's the matter?' Melanie asked, fearing her grandmother was about to tell her that she wasn't feeling well enough to continue.

'We can't go on the escalators,' her grandmother replied.

'Nonsense,' said Melanie. 'There's no problem. Hold my hand and you'll be fine.'

'No, no, no,' her grandmother was adamant. 'Look at the sign, Melanie. Look at the sign.'

Melanie peered in the direction that her grandmother was pointing, only to see that there, on one side of the escalator, was a small printed notice bearing the words: 'DOGS MUST BE CARRIED ON THE ESCALATORS.'

'We haven't got one,' Melanie's grandmother whispered.

Melanie, stifling her laughter, and not willing to point out that you didn't have to carry a dog every time you used the Underground, guided her grandmother to the stairs.

'On the way back we'll take a taxi, eh? It might be easier, mightn't it?' she said between giggles.

YOUTH OFFENDER

Most people are used to making silly mistakes and suffering the consequences, but sometimes when a senior moment strikes you, it is others who take the fall. This was the case when one young boy was summoned to appear before Bradford magistrates for driving offences. It transpired that the child, far from being a reckless driver, was in fact a law-abiding eleven-year-old.

Someone within the Bradford police force had suffered a senior moment, an explanation which the boy's father subsequently described as 'unbelievable'. However, as we all know, senior moments can strike at any time and, unlike Victor Meldrew, we *do* believe it!

A PLEASURABLE MEMORY

The poet Samuel Rogers was not only noted for giving large literary breakfasts and dinners, but also for his famous poem 'Pleasures of Memory', upon the publication of which a friend of Rogers came up to him and said, 'Lady X is dying to be introduced to the author of "Pleasures of Memory".'

'Pray let her live,' replied Rogers, crossing the room and approaching the lady.

'Mr Rogers, madam, author of "Pleasures of Memory",' his friend said, introducing the pair.

'Pleasures of what?' the woman asked.

MEDICAL MAYHEM

Nancy Metcalfe had never liked hospitals, so when she was informed that she needed an operation to remove her appendix, she was less than thrilled. Nevertheless, Nancy was in great pain and, with the threat hanging over her that her appendix might burst at any moment, she was only too grateful when she was rushed into the operating theatre.

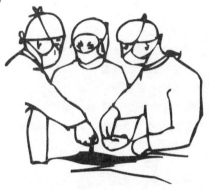

Afterwards, everything seemed to be fine. Nancy spent two days in hospital recuperating, then went home, where she spent a further few days in bed before returning to work. However, after a couple of weeks, Nancy started complaining of strange pains in her side, along with a general feeling of malaise. She went to her GP, who referred her to the hospital for X-rays. Only then was it discovered that the surgeon who had operated on her appendix, together with the attending nurses, had, while suffering a group senior moment, left a small medical instrument inside their patient. Nancy was rushed back into surgery, and, luckily for everyone involved, made a quick and full recovery.

IN THE NAME OF THE FATHER

The Irish poet and dramatist William Butler Yeats was fifty-four when his daughter, Anne, was born. Once, when Yeats and Anne got off a bus round the corner from where the family lived, Yeats turned and, not recognizing Anne for a moment as she approached the house, asked vaguely, 'Oh, and who is it you wish to see?'

NANNY STATE

During the police investigation into the murder of Sandra Rivett, the nanny of Lord Lucan's children, police came across a lady in Belgravia during their house-to-house enquiries. On hearing that Lucan had killed Rivett after having mistaken her for his wife, the woman replied: 'Oh dear, what a pity. Nannies are so hard to come by these days!'

MANEATER

Two old ladies, Hester and Ethel, were rocking in their chairs on the nursing-home porch. Hester said, 'Ethel, do you remember the minuet?'

Ethel replied, 'Oh God, I don't even remember the ones I slept with.'

DEAF EARS

One morning, a policeman pulled over an elderly driver on the M5 and said, 'My God, didn't you realize that your wife fell out of your car over five miles back?'

'Thank God!' said the driver.

'What do you mean, "Thank God"?' exclaimed the policeman in shock.

'Well, I thought I'd gone deaf,' replied the old gentleman.

DOCTOR'S ORDERS

According to an article that appeared in the *London Evening Standard* back in 1975, a doctor, whilst suffering from a seriously bad senior moment, threw all the drugs in his surgery into a large bucket and placed said bucket in the waiting room with this notice attached: 'HELP YOURSELVES. PLEASE DON'T BOTHER ME.'

Even when the General Medical Council reprimanded the doctor for serious misconduct, he didn't seem in the slightest bit bothered, replying that his treatment of his patients was no less random than that given out by other doctors!

TO RUSSIA WITH LOVE

Sometimes, even with the best of intentions, events can take a turn for the worse. Such was the case when a British businessman was sent by his company on a trade visit to Russia. Intent on making a good impression while he was over there, and knowing he had to give a keynote speech to a large gathering of Russian businessmen, the man dutifully wrote his speech, and afterwards had the whole piece translated phonetically into Russian, so that he could make the speech himself without the need of an intermediary.

When he arrived in Moscow, the businessman suddenly realized that he hadn't written his usual introductory piece and so did not know the Russian for 'Ladies and gentlemen'. However, being a quick thinker, the businessman headed straight for the lavatories when he reached his hotel. When he saw women going in through one door and men through another, he duly noted down what was written on the sign outside each and put these words at the beginning of his talk.

The speech went exceedingly well indeed; the crowd were in raptures; when the businessman had finished his talk, he was given a standing ovation, presumably because he had spoken in Russian throughout.

'There is just one thing that is bothering us,' said one delegate. 'Why is it that at the beginning of the speech you chose to address us as "Urinals and Water Closets"?'

BLOOMING AWFUL

Senior moments don't come much more painful than the following incident, which affected Violet Manning when, on going out into her garden without her spectacles to collect some shallots for that night's meal of coq au vin, she dug up a handful of daffodil bulbs instead. Not realizing her mistake, she chopped up the bulbs, lightly fried them in butter, then later that day served up the meal to her family, who promptly all came down with food poisoning. Luckily no one was seriously injured, although two members of the family weren't allowed out of hospital for a few days.

MILITARY MISHAP

It's not just us mere mortals who are prone to the odd senior moment or two – the likes of the British military have also experienced their fair share of silly blunders, as the following story testifies.

Having ploughed a vast amount of money into a new anti-aircraft gun, which was designed to shoot down helicopters by targeting the machine's rotating blades, the British government was forced to abandon the project when, during a test of the system, the gun zeroed in on a nearby bathroom exhaust fan that was mounted on the outside of a building. Everybody had to be evacuated from the premises and no one was hurt, except perhaps the gun's designer, whose pride must have been well and truly battered.

SPENDING HABIT

During his time in the White House, John F. Kennedy found a piece of paper with the reminder 'Department store – $40,000' written on it. Immediately recognizing his wife's writing, and aware of Jackie's spendthrift habits, he confronted his wife.

'What the hell is this?' he quizzed her. Jackie glanced down at the note, considered for a moment, and said, 'I don't remember.'

ONE DRINK TOO MANY

One evening in December 2006, Lancaster police received an emergency phone call from a man at the Duke of Westminster's country estate in the Trough of Bowland. Having broken into the Duke's house, the man had discovered a drinks cabinet containing three bottles of claret, which he knocked back in quick succession. Drunk and disorderly, the burglar then made his way through to the kitchen to cook himself a meal. Turning on the gas cooker, he failed to notice that he hadn't actually lit the appliance. The room quickly filled with gas, but the man, oblivious to the hazard, continued to potter around until a stray spark ignited the building. Miraculously, the thief survived, but he had to call for the fire brigade to dig him out of the rubble.

DUMB AND DUMBER

Police in Marked Tree, Arkansas, were astonished at how easy it was to track down a thief after he attempted to rob an Arkansas bank. The robber, Michael Brown, having broken into the bank after it had closed, found there was no money for him to steal, so instead took a portable radio and a huge handful of sweets.

When police arrived at the bank, they found a trail of sweet wrappers all the way down the street, across a railroad track, straight into a trailer park where Brown was living at the time. Upon Brown's arrest, police discovered that he was also wanted on charges of breaking into a local jewellery store. He had taken a tray of rings from a display case, however all of the items turned out to be plastic . . .

YOU'VE BEEN GRADED

During his early career as a theatrical agent, television impresario Lew Grade once went backstage after a show at the Finsbury Park Empire in order to meet one of the acts he'd particularly enjoyed.

'That was fantastic,' he enthused. 'How much are you being paid?'

The act replied that they were getting only twenty-five pounds a week.

'You're joking,' replied Grade. 'If you signed up with me, I could get you at least forty pounds a week. Who's your agent?'

The reply, when it came, made even Grade blush.

'You are,' they answered.

COUNTING THE YEARS

'I'm sixty-three and I guess that puts me in with geriatrics, but if there were fifteen months in every year, I'd be only forty-three.'

– JAMES THURBER, COMEDIAN AND CARTOONIST

PARTING WORDS

The older a man gets, the more ways he learns to part his hair. Some men pull around what little bit of hair they have on their head to cover their baldness. However, as a man gets even older, he realizes there are basically only three ways to wear his hair – parted, unparted and departed.

FARMYARD FROLICS

A Dutch vet was fined £140 for setting light to and subsequently burning down a farm with a jet of flame from the rear end of a cow. Apparently the vet was trying to test the cow's gas levels, but had obviously not thought the problem through carefully when he lit a match and caused nearby hay bales to catch on fire. The estimated cost of the damage was £45,000. The cow was thankfully unharmed, while the vet was extremely embarrassed.

ARMED AND DANGEROUS

In Florida it was reported that an elderly woman, having done some shopping at the supermarket, returned to the car park to find four men in the process of driving off in her car. Dropping her shopping bags on the ground, the octogenarian pulled out a handgun from her rear pocket and screamed at the men: 'I have a gun and I know how to use it! Get out of the car!'

Much to her surprise, the four men did exactly as she demanded and quickly ran from the vehicle out of the car park. Loading her bags into the car, the old lady, still shaking from the experience, got into the driving seat and tried to put her key in the ignition, but no matter how many times she tried to do so, the key wouldn't fit. Suddenly, the old lady realized her mistake.

Getting out of the car and unloading her bags, she found her own car parked only a few spaces down, after which she drove straight to the nearest police station. The sergeant on the front desk could hardly contain his laughter when she told him what had happened, for who should be standing at the far side of the interview room, but four very shaken-looking men who had just reported a carjacking. And the assailant? An elderly female with white hair, sporting glasses and wielding a huge handgun!

RECOVERY TIME

'You're getting older when it takes you more time to recover than it did to tire you out.'
— MILTON BERLE, COMEDIAN

IDENTITY CRISIS

One day, a nurse entered the geriatric ward, only to be told that the patient in bed three was being discharged that morning. On seeing an elderly gentleman sitting on the bed, already fully dressed and with his suitcase packed neatly beside him, the nurse went up to explain the hospital rules, namely that all patients had to use a wheelchair to leave the building when they were discharged. The old gentleman, Joseph, insisted he didn't need a wheelchair to take him downstairs, but the nurse was having none of it, so eventually he gave up and seated himself in the contraption. On the way down, the nurse and Joseph chatted away, during which time the nurse asked Joseph if his wife was meeting him in the car park.

'Oh no,' said Joseph, 'June's still upstairs in the bathroom getting changed into her own clothes. She really hated that hospital gown.'

'An old-timer is someone who can remember when a naughty child was taken to the woodshed instead of to a psychiatrist.'
– DAVID GREENBERG, AUTHOR

'From birth to age eighteen, a girl needs good parents. From eighteen to thirty-five, she needs good looks. From thirty-five to fifty-five, she needs a good personality. From fifty-five on, she needs good cash.'
– SOPHIE TUCKER, SINGER AND COMEDIAN

DAYDREAMER

The eighteenth-century philosopher, Adam Smith, was a quiet soul who was so forgetful that one day he left his garden and, deep in philosophical thought, walked twelve miles to Dunfermline. Once there, he was roused from his daydreaming by the sound of the town's church bells, at which point he glanced down, only to realize he'd come out wearing nothing but a nightgown.

LET THERE BE LIGHT

Canon Dr Graham Kings, aged fifty-three, must have been suffering a senior moment when, having lit a few candles around the pulpit in his church of St Mary's, Islington, north London, the flames subsequently set fire to his sermon! Unfortunately for him, his mistake was caught on camera and afterwards posted on YouTube, where the clip has received thousands of hits.

MEDICAL MISHAPS

In *Mould's Medical Anecdotes*, R. F. Mould lists a whole gamut of replies to a circular from a chiropody clinic asking if patients would like transport to and from their appointments. Here are just a few:

- My husband is dead and will not bring me.

- I have arthritis of the spine and can hardly walk into doors.

- I can't use my legs or my wife's.

- I can't breathe and haven't done so for many years.

- My mother is ninety-six and must have a car as she has got long fingernails.

- I live five miles from clinic and postman says I should have it.

- I suffer from thyroid and cannot climb as I don't have a car.

- I cannot walk up a hill unless it is down and the hill to the clinic is up.

- I must have your transport. We have a car but my husband is seventy-six and I haven't had it for a long time.

- I am blind in one eye and my leg.

SHE DRIVES ME CRAZY

An old codger called Charlie was getting married aged eighty-nine. His friend Fred, a year or so older, asked him if his wife-to-be was pretty.

'No,' replied Charlie.

'Is she a good cook?'

'No,' replied Charlie.

'Is she very rich?'

Again Charlie answered with a negative.

'She must be very good in bed then?'

'I've no idea,' Charlie replied.

'So why on earth are you marrying her?'

'She can still drive at night.'

FROM BEYOND THE GRAVE

Philip Gosse, author of the beautiful, semi-autobiographical *Father and Son,* was a good friend of the poet Algernon Charles Swinburne. One day, shortly after Swinburne's sad demise, Gosse's maid burst into a room in which her boss was entertaining friends.

'Mr Swinburne to speak to you on the telephone, sir!' the woman exclaimed. To which Gosse, never one to miss a humorous moment, replied: 'Mr Swinburne to speak to me on the telephone? I shall certainly not speak to Mr Swinburne. I don't know where he may be calling from.'

NO WHINING PLEASE

A New York wine merchant by the name of William Sokolin was once commissioned by an anonymous wine collector to sell at auction a bottle of Chateau Margaux 1787 that had once been owned by Thomas Jefferson. The price of the bottle was set by Sokolin at a whopping $500,000, but when the auction took place, the bottle didn't sell.

Sokolin dejectedly carried himself and the bottle off to dinner at the Four Seasons restaurant. After a beautiful meal, disaster struck. A waiter, who was perhaps a little tired after a long shift, chose this opportunity to suffer a senior moment. Carrying a tray past Sokolin's table, the young man knocked over the bottle of wine, which crashed to the floor and broke. Of course, the bottle was insured, but unfortunately for William Sokolin and the bottle's owner, for only half the price it had been put up for at auction.

'It has been said that there is no fool like an old fool, except a young fool. But the young fool has first to grow up to be an old fool to realize what a damn fool he was when he was a young fool.'
— Harold Macmillan, politician

'Time and tide wait for no man, but time always stands still
for a woman of thirty.'
– ROBERT FROST, POET

RICH MAN

The aptly named entertainer Harry Richman was occasionally known to tip a waiter fifty dollars simply for being handed the menu. Richman once asked a head waiter, 'What's the biggest tip you've ever received?'

'A hundred dollars,' the waiter replied. Richman gave the man two hundred dollars.

'Now tell me,' Richman asked, 'who gave you the hundred?'

'You did, Mr Richman,' the waiter replied.

COOKING UP TROUBLE

According to Robert Paterson in his book *The Monarch Book of Christian Wisdom*, when Archbishop Richard Chenevix Trench returned to his old parish in Dublin to visit Lord Plunkett, who was to succeed him, his memory was a little the worse for wear. For upon sitting down to lunch with his host, he forgot that it wasn't him giving the meal.

Turning to his wife, the archbishop is said to have remarked, 'I'm afraid, my love, that we must put this cook down among our failures.'

> **YOU KNOW YOU'RE GETTING OLD WHEN . . .**
> ' . . . everything takes longer to do – bathing, shaving,
> getting dressed or undressed – but when time passes
> quickly, as if he were gathering speed while
> coasting downhill.'
> – MALCOLM COWLEY, WRITER

WHOSE FRIEND ARE YOU, ANYWAY?

Matthew had never thought of himself as the type of man to suffer a senior moment. After all, he was only twenty-six years old and in the prime of life. He was far too young to experience awful indignities such as forgetting where he'd last seen his glasses or the name of his best friend. However, one rainy, blustery day while standing in a long queue of people for a bus, the worst happened. Feeling cold and bedraggled, Matthew was cursing the fact that he didn't have enough money to catch a taxi home when, out of the blue, he saw one of his friends, a girl called Marjorie, drive past in her car. Marjorie was slowing down so that Matthew, seeing the opportunity for a lift, began running after the vehicle.

'Marjorie! Marjorie!' he shouted, waving his arms about in the air.

Eventually, the car stopped and Matthew opened the door and jumped in. Only then did he realize his mistake. The car wasn't being driven by Marjorie at all, but by a lady who began shrieking at him to get out of her vehicle.

'Police!' she screamed. 'Help! Help!'

Matthew, covered in confusion, made his apologies along with a very quick exit, only to be met by the disapproving stares of the entire bus queue! Too embarrassed to join them again, he then had to walk all the way home in the rain.

A SHAW THING

The playwright George Bernard Shaw was also a noted theatre critic in his time. One day, while watching a play that he was supposed to be reviewing for the *London Saturday Review*, Shaw suffered a senior moment, which he explained thus:

I am in a somewhat foolish position concerning a play at the *Opera Comique*, whither I was bidden this day week. For some reason I was not supplied with a program; so that I never learned the name of the play. At the end of the second act, the play had advanced about as far as an ordinary dramatist would have brought it five minutes after the first rising of the curtain; or, say, as far as Ibsen would have brought it ten years before that event. Taking advantage of the second interval to stroll out into the Strand for a little exercise, I unfortunately forgot all about my business, and actually reached home before it occurred to me that I had not seen the end of the play. Under these circumstances, it would ill become me to dogmatize on the merits of the work or its performance. I can only offer the management my apologies.

BORN AGAIN

A man's death was mistakenly noted in the local paper's obituary section. The 'corpse' hastened to the editor to protest. 'I'm awfully sorry,' the editor replied. 'But it's too late to do much about it. The best thing I can do for you is to put you in the "Birth Column" tomorrow morning to give you a fresh start!'

WHAT A DOPE

The following true story may be an example of a chronic senior moment or sheer stupidity or both. Often, the two go hand in hand: senior moments frequently occur when we fail to think something through to its logical conclusion. This was surely the case when a young man decided to put photos of his brother's prized marijuana plants on his MySpace page, thus alerting police to his illegal activities. The man was subsequently arrested and charged with felony distribution after police employed an undercover agent to pose as a buyer.

> 'You're only young once, but you can be immature all your life.'
> – CHARLES E. SCOGGINS, WRITER

THE NAME GAME

We all try our best to avoid senior moments. Some of us write lists or notes on the backs of our hands so as not to forget something important, whilst others ensure that they have at least sixteen sets of house keys hidden strategically around their property, so that they never find themselves locked out. However, for sheer gall, nothing quite beats the audacity or cunning of the man who admitted that he called all his girlfriends (at the time he had four) by the same nickname. This meant that he never made the mistake of waking up with one and calling her the wrong name. How's that for prevention being better than a cure?

MISSPELLED YOUTH

When the British poet and journalist J. C. Squire wrote an article about *A Midsummer Night's Dream*, he was somewhat amused to discover that the typesetter, in a moment of senioritis, had misspelled the name 'Hermia' and written 'Hernia' instead. Squire opted to leave the misspelling as it was, saying: 'I cannot bring myself to interfere with my printer's first fine careless rupture.'

CLINTON'S CATASTROPHE

Next time you are suffering a senior moment, just be glad that world peace and security do not depend upon you keeping your wits about you. For poor old Bill Clinton, the consequences of even the smallest of memory lapses were once potentially dire. The former US president once suffered a chronic senior moment when he left perhaps the most important piece of luggage in the world – the 'nuclear football' – at a NATO summit meeting.

The 'nuclear football' is a briefcase that contains all of America's nuclear-bomb codes. Containing the electronic launch codes required for a US nuclear strike, the case also provides a link with

the Pentagon through a telephone. It is carried by and chained to a military aide and it is supposed to be near the president whenever he is away from the White House. The black attaché case has been passed from president to president since the days of Dwight Eisenhower and has been called the most dangerous handbag in the world. In this particular instance, when President Clinton's motorcade left without him, the aide who carried the briefcase then had to walk the half-mile back to the White House from the Reagan building where the summit had been held. 'We're safe,' remarked Joe Lockhart, the president's spokesman, following the arrival of the aide, adding, 'These things happen.' Indeed, other presidents have had similar scares: Jimmy Carter left codes in his suit when it was sent to the dry cleaners; the case was left on board Air Force One in Paris when Gerald Ford arrived at an economic summit; and the 'nuclear football' was separated from Ronald Reagan when he was shot in 1981.

JAILHOUSE ROCK

Most of us at some time or another have had to give a speech, be it at a wedding or for work purposes, but hopefully none of us have made such an enormous gaffe as the English Labour politician Chuter Ede (1882–1965) when he visited a prison in order to make a speech to the inmates. According to Lord Elwyn-Jones, who related this anecdote on BBC Radio 4's *Quote . . . Unquote* programme, Ede began his speech with the immortal words, 'I'm so glad to see you all here . . . '

UPSTAIRS, DOWNSTAIRS

'The memory's going so I go up and down the stairs a lot. I go upstairs, I remember something downstairs; I go down again, I forget what I'm doing. I go into the garden, I forget what I'm there for. Then I have to stand in the same place and think, "Why am I here?"'
– MICHELE HANSON, JOURNALIST

SENIOR SOLACE

Most of the time when we experience a senior moment it is because we ourselves have done something stupid, however occasionally it is because the opposite occurs – that is to say, because someone else is suffering a senior moment, as the following two examples attest.

Dear Sir,

Upon the death of my mother, I informed all the appropriate utilities. I was somewhat surprised to receive a reply, addressed to my mother, from British Gas. 'Dear Mrs Pack (deceased), can you please explain the reason for failing to pay your most recent bill.'

Corinne Taylor, Essex – *THE WEEK* MAGAZINE, DECEMBER 2006

Dear Sir,

My wife has just received a letter from the government's pension service. It began: 'Dear Mrs J. Goodison, I am sorry to hear that Sir Nicholas Goodison has died and would like to express my sympathy to you.' It told her that my winter fuel payment of £100 (for which I qualified because I was alive in September) would be sent to her bank account.

I called the pension service and discovered that my state pension had also been 'suspended' because I had 'passed away'.

I should have known this would happen when I died – the pension service's notes do say that 'if your circumstances change, it may affect any payment you get'.

I wonder what killed me? Was I a victim of a Treasury plan to restrain the growth of state borrowing, or of its increasing dictation of the little details of our lives?

Sir Nicholas Goodison – *THE WEEK* MAGAZINE, DECEMBER 2006

COMMON SCENTS

There is an esteemed actor who, due to old age, has great difficulty remembering his lines. After many years, he finds a theatre where they are prepared to give him a chance to shine again.

The director says, 'This is the most important part of the play, and it requires only one line. You must walk on to the stage at the play's opening carrying a rose. You hold the rose to your nose with just one finger and thumb, sniff the rose deeply and then speak the line, "Ah, the sweet aroma of my mistress." '

The actor is excited to be back on stage. All day long, before the play opens, he practises his line over and over again.

Finally, the moment of the performance arrives. The curtain rises and the actor walks on to the stage. Using just one finger, he delivers the line with poignancy, 'Ah, the sweet aroma of my mistress.'

The theatre erupts, the audience screams with laughter and the director is furious.

'You incompetent idiot!' he cries. 'You have ruined me!'

The actor is bewildered. 'What's wrong, did I forget my line?'

'No!' yells the director. 'You forgot the rose!'

LATTER-DAY LAZARUS

Gravediggers and mourners alike were horrified when, during the funeral of a man in Venezuela in the 1970s, the corpse suddenly sprang back to life and jumped out of its coffin. Unfortunately, the shock of seeing this latter-day Lazarus was too much for one woman at the funeral, who promptly collapsed and died from a heart attack. She was later buried in the grave that had been prepared for the 'dead' man, but only after doctors – who had obviously been suffering a serious case of senior momentitus when they signed the man's death certificate – had made absolutely certain that there wasn't a mistake second time round.

Another apocryphal tale concerns a GP who was summoned to a house in which one of his patients had recently passed away. The GP pronounced the man dead, after which all the necessary arrangements were made for a wake. The GP was in attendance, as was the dead man's family, a nurse, priest and, of course, the dead man himself, whose body was laid in an open coffin for all to see. The drink flowed and people reminisced about their dearly departed friend until, all of a sudden, the dead man sat bold upright in his coffin and said, 'Is this a private party or can anyone join in?'

Sadly, on being informed what had happened, the man suffered a massive heart attack and dropped dead for a second time. The wake continued and a couple of days later, the man was buried.

'Old age is an excellent time for outrage. My goal is to say or do at least one outrageous thing every week.'
– MAGGIE KUHN, ACTIVIST

MEMORY LANE

'No woman should have a memory. Memory in a woman
is the beginning of dowdiness.'
– OSCAR WILDE, WRITER

ON THE MENU

A ninety-year-old man checked into a posh hotel
to celebrate his birthday. As a surprise, a few of
his friends sent a call girl to his room. When the
man opened the door, he saw before him a
beautiful young woman.

She said, 'I've brought you a present.'
The old man replied, 'What is it?'
She said, 'I am yours for super sex.'
He said, 'I'm ninety years old, I'll have the
soup.'

THE YOUTH OF TODAY

'The denunciation of the young is a necessary part of
the hygiene of older people, and greatly assists the
circulation of the blood.'
– LOGAN PEARSALL SMITH, WRITER

DOWN ON ONE KNEE

When eighty-four-year-old William fell in love with his eighty-three-year-old neighbour Phyllis, he thought his heart would burst with joy. However, little did he know that it was another part of his body that would give way first. Getting down on his knees to propose to Phyllis, he told her that he wanted to ask her two questions. Firstly, would she marry him?

'Oh, yes,' she replied. 'But what's your second question?'

'Will you help me up?'

SPACE-AGE DEFECT

If you were a mechanic, you might be excused the odd senior moment when, for example, you forgot to check the oil in a car's engine or to top up the water. But if you're dealing with spacecraft, mistakes of this nature can be a little more costly.

When Mariner 1 (which was intended to fly all the way to Venus in order to collect valuable data and send it back to Earth) was launched at Cape Canaveral on 22 July 1962, a hardware failure occurred, which caused the on-board computer to assume control of the craft.

The person who had been responsible for keying the correct data into the computer had obviously been suffering a terrible senior moment, for they had unwittingly missed keying in the superscript bar, which meant the computer's software was faulty. A few minutes after its launch, the rocket veered dangerously off course and had to be destroyed. Not a good day for America.

ROYAL GAFFE

During her wedding to Prince Charles, Lady Diana Spencer suffered a senior moment at the tender age of nineteen, and vowed: 'I, Diana Frances, take thee, Philip Charles Arthur George, to be my wedded husband' – accidentally mixing up Charles's first two names. However, Prince Charles then went on to vow generously, 'All thy goods with thee I share,' instead of the traditional and correct, 'All *my* goods with thee I share . . . '

VERBAL DIARRHOEA

In 1949, Macdonald Hobley, a TV announcer of the day, had the job of introducing the then Chancellor of the Exchequer, Sir Stafford Cripps. Sat in Studio A at Alexandra Palace with Cripps at his side, Hobley piped up with the glorious and legendary introduction: 'Here to speak on behalf of the Labour Party is Sir Stifford Crapps . . . '

ANIMAL MATTERS

When it comes to looking after other people's pets, there is so much scope for senior moments that it is hard to know which of the many available anecdotes to put in this book, but one story, no doubt based on an urban legend, seems more fitting than most.

Mrs Heyworth was asked by her neighbours, who were going away to America for a month's holiday, to look after their children's animals. The neighbours left and Mrs Heyworth conscientiously looked after Charlie, the children's dog, and Hamish, the children's hamster, feeding both animals every day. One morning, Charlie bounded into the house carrying the neighbours' pet rabbit in his mouth. Mrs Heyworth was beside herself. She had completely forgotten that this animal existed and hadn't fed him at all; now the dog had killed him and brought his bruised and bloody body into the house.

Panicking slightly, Mrs Heyworth decided the best thing to do was to clean the rabbit up, put it back in its cage, and hope that her neighbours, on their return, would think that the animal had died naturally in its sleep. Some days later, Mrs Heyworth received a rather puzzled call from her friends, thanking her for looking after the dog and the hamster, but wondering why the rabbit, which had died the day before they went on holiday and had been buried in their garden, was now rotting in its cage?

HANDS UP

You would think that when a group of people decide to rob a bank, they would have planned the event meticulously in advance, covering all eventualities. But this wasn't the case for one group of hapless, Scottish bank robbers, who were suffering a collective senior moment when they set out one day to hold up a bank. Arriving at the building, the first thing to go wrong was that all three men got stuck in the revolving doors and had to be helped free by members of staff. Not put off by this mishap, the men eventually entered the bank and demanded that the employees hand over £5,000 in cash. By this time, the head cashier couldn't take the threat seriously (in fact, she thought the whole thing was a practical joke) and she burst into laughter along with her colleagues. Somewhat downcast by this reaction, the head robber subsequently reduced his demand for £5,000 to £500, then to £50 and finally to 50 pence. And the humiliation didn't end there. One of the robbers, growing fed up with the cashiers' refusal to take the robbery seriously, decided to jump over the counter and fetch the money for himself.

Sadly, however, he didn't get very far as having launched himself on to the counter, he fell over and twisted his ankle. Finally, the robbers made their getaway, but not before first getting stuck in the revolving doors again on their way out.

HOW DO YOU INSURE AGAINST STUPIDITY?

Whether the following accidents were caused by senior moments cannot be verified, but what can be proved is that, when writing out the insurance claims, certain people need to check they're not suffering early senile dementia.

- The guy was all over the road. I had to swerve a number of times before I hit him.

- Going to work at 7 a.m. this morning, I drove out of my drive straight into a bus. The bus was five minutes early.

- The pedestrian had no idea which way to go, so I ran him over.

- The other car collided with mine without giving warning of its intention.

- The car in front of me hit the pedestrian, but he got up so I hit him again.

- Coming home, I drove into the wrong house and collided with a tree I didn't have.

- I was driving along when I saw two kangaroos copulating in the middle of the road, causing me to ejaculate through the sunroof.

- I pulled into the side of the road because there was smoke coming from under the hood. I realized that there was a fire in the engine, so I took my dog and smothered it with a blanket.

- I didn't think that the speed limit applied after midnight.

- I started to slow down, but the traffic was more stationary than I thought.

- I thought that my window was down, but I found it was up when I put my hand through it.

- I was driving my car out of the driveway in the usual manner when it was struck by the other car in the same place it had been struck several times before.

- I knew that my dog was possessive about the car, but I would not have asked her to drive it if I had thought there was any risk.

- I was unable to stop in time and my car crashed into the other vehicle. The driver and passengers then left immediately for a vacation with injuries.

- I had been shopping for plants all day and was on my way home. As I reached an intersection, a hedge sprang up, obscuring my vision, and I did not see the other car.

- I was thrown from the car as it left the road. I was later found in a ditch by some stray cows.

- My car was legally parked as it backed into another vehicle.

- The pedestrian ran for the pavement, but I got him.

- The accident occurred when I was attempting to bring my car out of a skid by steering it into the other vehicle.

- I had been driving for forty years when I fell asleep at the wheel and had an accident.

- An invisible car came out of nowhere, struck my car and vanished.

- The indirect cause of the accident was a little guy in a small car with a big mouth.

- I pulled away from the side of the road, glanced at my mother-in-law and headed over the embankment.

- I had been learning to drive with power steering. I turned the wheel to what I thought was enough and found myself in a different direction going the opposite way.

- The telephone pole was approaching fast. I was attempting to swerve out of its path when it struck my front end.

- When I saw I could not avoid a collision, I stepped on the gas and crashed into the other car.

HOT AIR AND TOILET PAPER

When the owner of Virgin Atlantic and Virgin Records, Sir Richard Branson, was interviewed after one of his epic balloon journeys and asked what, if any, tips he would have for other would-be adventurers, he is said to have replied: 'If you're embarking around the world in a hot-air balloon, don't forget the toilet paper. Once, we had to wait for incoming faxes.'

ARTISTIC LICENCE

It is common knowledge that artists are known for their eccentricity and lack of practical ability when it comes to everyday matters. One apocryphal tale perfectly illustrates this phenomenon.

A German artist, renowned for his forgetfulness, was at a party at the house of a close acquaintance. His host, who was also an artist, began talking about a recently published book on Vermeer, a painter dear to both men. Unwilling to leave his guests alone, the host asked his friend to go up to the master bedroom, where, he said, he would find the book on the bedside table and should bring it downstairs.

So the artist went upstairs to the master bedroom, but when he got there, it seems he forgot his purpose entirely and, instead of finding the book and taking it downstairs to the drawing room, he climbed into the enormous bed, where he promptly fell asleep. A bemused guest found him an hour later, still fast asleep. It appears that the artist had thought he was in his own house and, feeling a little tired and just a tad disoriented, had decided to have an early night. Talk about making yourself at home.

GRANTED

Actor Hugh Grant claims that he is now finding it difficult to remember his lines. Says Hugh: 'I start to sweat like a wolf, my tongue swells to twice its normal size, my brain seizes up and I dry.' How very painful!

> 'Retirement must be wonderful. I mean, you can suck in your stomach for only so long.'
> – BURT REYNOLDS, ACTOR

POLICE WITNESS

Senior moments can sometimes strike the very young indeed, as the following anecdote illustrates. *Samuel Butler's Notebooks* records the story of a law student who was asked in a *viva voce* examination what was necessary to render a marriage legal in Scotland. The student replied: 'For a marriage to be valid in Scotland, it is absolutely necessary that it should be consummated in the presence of two policemen.'

A HELPFUL HUSBAND

Seventy-year-old Mrs Jones went to the doctor for her annual check-up. He told her that she needed more activity and recommended sex three times a week. She said to the doctor, 'Please, tell my husband.' The doctor went out to the waiting room and told Mr Jones that his wife needed to have sex three times a week. Her eighty-year-old husband replied, 'Which days?'

'How about Monday, Wednesday and Friday?'

'I can bring her in on Monday and Wednesday,' the man said, 'but on Friday she'll have to take the bus.'

RECAPTURED YOUTH

'When I meet old fans, I swear that I can see the girls they were – the wrinkles vanish. That so many people respond to me is fabulous. It is like having a kind of Alzheimer's disease, where everyone knows you and you don't know anyone.'

– TONY CURTIS, ACTOR

MILKING IT

There can be barely anyone who hasn't woken up in the morning and gone downstairs to breakfast only to find that there is no milk left in the fridge for their tea, coffee or cereal. This is precisely what happened to Millie Brown, aged fifty-four, from Woking in Surrey. However, far from being a minor inconvenience, this 'no milk' scenario ended up costing a bomb.

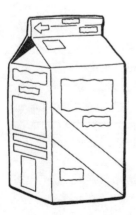

Having checked the fridge, and realizing that her husband must have finished the last few drops before he went into work, Millie got dressed and headed for the shops. Halfway to the precinct, she realized that she had come out without her house keys. It was winter and all the windows to the house were closed so Millie, knowing her husband always carried a set of keys himself, found a phone box and rang him up at his office.

'I'm so glad you rang,' he said. 'I was going to call you in a minute. I've forgotten my keys so can you make sure you're in when I get home tonight?'

Millie didn't have the heart to tell her husband that she'd just locked herself out, so instead she reassured him that she'd be there and, having chatted to him for a couple of minutes, put the phone down before calling a locksmith.

One hour later, the locksmith arrived and proceeded to break into the house (it took him less than fifteen seconds to complete the procedure), after which Millie asked him if he'd like a cup of tea.

'No, thank you,' the locksmith replied, handing her an invoice for £110 plus VAT. 'Got to get to my next job.'

'No matter,' said Millie wanly. 'I haven't got any milk, anyway.'

BODYSNATCHER

Senior moments aren't just confined to having problems remembering things – often a senior moment is experienced when you realize your body is not quite what it once was: 'I don't actually inhabit my body any more. At some point somebody came along, bodysnatched, gave me this. It's the kind of body I used to look at on beaches and think, "Goodness me, how does that happen? How could you let yourself go like that?" That's how it happens – it just happens.'

– KATHRYN FLETT, WRITER

SPOONERISMS

University professors are notorious for their absent-mindedness, but for sheer senility few can surpass the Reverend William Spooner, of spoonerism fame, who in the first quarter of the twentieth century was Warden of New College, Oxford.

On one occasion, having bumped into someone he didn't recognize in the college quad, Spooner asked the gentleman to join a party he was giving the following day to welcome the new mathematics fellow to the team.

'I *am* the new mathematics fellow,' the man said.

'Oh dear! Never mind. Come along anyway,' replied Spooner.

Another occasion saw Spooner preaching a sermon, at the end of which he announced, 'In the sermon I have just preached, whenever I said Aristotle, I meant St Paul.'

And finally, there is the wonderful tale of when Spooner bumped into one of his undergraduate students in Oxford. Greeting Dr Spooner, the young man said, 'I don't suppose you remember me?' To which Spooner is supposed to have replied: 'Of course, I remember your name perfectly, but I've completely forgotten your face.'

AGEING GRACEFULLY

'Getting older is fabulous. The longer you do it, the more technique you acquire. That makes the game easier.'

– CHERI LUNGHI, ACTRESS

'Old age is no place for sissies.'
– BETTE DAVIS, ACTRESS

THE STORY OF YO-YO AND THE CELLO

World-famous musicians are not renowned for having
many senior moments, but Yo-Yo Ma will probably go
down in history not only for being one of the most
celebrated cellists of all time, but also for losing his
prized instrument while on a trip to New York. The
mishap occurred when Ma was taking a taxi ride
after playing at Carnegie Hall. He got out of the
cab, leaving the three-hundred-year-old cello
(nicknamed Petunia) behind in the vehicle!
Estimated to be worth around 2.5 million dollars, the
instrument was later recovered without a scratch on it.

STEAL AWAY

If you are going to rob a bank, it is probably best not to have a
senior moment whilst you're on the job, as one hapless robber
discovered to his detriment.

On successfully holding up the bank in question, the burglar
left the building, only to discover that he didn't know how to get

out of town. He asked directions from a passer-by, who unfortunately happened to be related to the bank manager and had already been alerted to the robbery. Thinking that the man fitted the description of the thief, the boy immediately phoned the police.

Shortly afterwards, the thief was arrested and charged with second-degree robbery.

SENIOR VIRUS

Human beings are not the only victims of senior moments. In Sweden, in the early 1980s, a computer effectively killed off thousands of people from Boraas county records when an operator asked it to update its records regarding recent deaths. Owing to a numerical error, the computer proceeded to wipe all records of the citizens' lives from its memory banks, causing mayhem in the affected area.

SEIZE THE DAY

'Hold fast to time! Use it! Be conscious of each day, each hour! They slip away unnoticed all too easily and swiftly.'
– THOMAS MANN, WRITER

MISTAKEN IDENTITY

One evening, the author P. G. Wodehouse was sitting next to an elderly woman at dinner when she began lavishly praising him for his books. According to the woman, her sons were huge fans of his work; they always bought his latest novels and their rooms were lined with copies of all his books. 'And when I tell them,' she concluded, 'that I have actually been sitting at dinner with Edgar Wallace, I don't know what they will say.'

WHAT A LOAD OF RUBBISH!

When the sixteenth-century mathematician Charles Cavendish died in 1654, he left his wife a huge collection of incredibly rare mathematical tomes that he had collected from all over Europe in manuscript form. His wife, however, not realizing their value, and fed up of storing such a lot of paper, sold the lot 'by weight' for wastepaper!

HIRSUTES YOU, SIR

Senior moments often result in shame and embarrassment. Think, for example, of those times when you are searching for your false teeth and someone is ringing on the doorbell, or when you can't find your glasses and someone kindly points out that you are wearing them. But the following anecdote is perhaps an indignity too far.

The TV broadcaster and journalist Reginald Bosanquet was filming in Africa when he had to stoop down to enter a small mud hut. His cameraman, who was following closely behind, suddenly felt something unusual lying at his feet. The object appeared to be large and furry and, in order to get it away from him, he began kicking and stamping on it, only to hear Bosanquet shouting for him to get off his toupee, which now lay ruined in the dust.

HASTY EXIT

South Dakota senator Larry Pressler once attempted to leave a Commerce Committee meeting, but somehow managed to confuse one door with another and entered a storage cupboard. Pressler was so mortified that he decided to remain in the cupboard until his colleagues left the room via the correct exit. It had not occurred to Pressler that the other senators had just witnessed his mistake and were waiting to greet him when he shuffled out, ensuring that this gargantuan gaffe was widely reported thereafter.

SENIOR ROMANCE

A well-dressed gentleman in his mid-nineties walks into a smart cocktail lounge and spies an elegant lady in her mid-eighties at the bar.

The gentleman walks over, sits alongside the old lady, orders a drink, takes a sip, turns to her and says, 'So, tell me, do I come here often?'

DUDLEY'S INVITATION

Clergyman and author Sydney Smith once noted of Lord Dudley that he was 'one of the most absent [-minded] men I have ever met with in society. One day he met me in the street and invited me to meet myself: "Dine with me today; dine with me, and I will get Sydney Smith to meet you." I admitted the temptation he held out to me, but said I was engaged to meet him elsewhere.'

SELECTIVE MEMORY

'I did not cry, I seldom laughed and did not make a noise; at four, I was caught putting salt in the jam, out of scientific interest rather than devilment, I suppose, anyway, it is the only crime I can remember.'

– JEAN-PAUL SARTRE, PHILOSOPHER

DEAD MAN WALKING

Remembering people's names is not always as easy as one would like, but the following anecdote, related by broadcaster Brian Johnston in *I Say, I Say, I Say*, shows that recalling a name is sometimes only half the battle.

'An ancient and rather doddery headmaster prided himself on his memory and always boasted that he could remember anyone's name. At an old boys' gathering, he went up to one of them and said, "You are Smith Minor, if I remember right."

"Yes, sir, I am. How clever of you to recognize me."

"Tell me, Smith, was it you or your brother who was killed in the war?"'

LIGHTS, CAMERA, ACTION!

The renowned producer Cecil B. DeMille, who is probably best remembered for his huge biblical epics, was one day filming a battle scene, which involved hundreds of thousands of extras plus several truckloads of animals. It was the type of scene that, once completed, could never be filmed again owing to the more than likely fact that the entire set would be destroyed during the ensuing mayhem. In order to ensure that the whole thing was captured in the first and only take, DeMille insisted on having four cameramen filming the battle from different angles.

When the scene was finished and the set destroyed, DeMille went to each of the cameramen in turn to ask what they had shot. The first cameraman explained rather sheepishly that his equipment had jammed and therefore he hadn't caught anything. The second cameraman said he'd had a hair in the gate and therefore his footage was ruined, while the third cameraman had to confess that the sun had shone into his lens and, like his two friends, he had managed to capture nothing. DeMille, desperate for some good news, then turned expectantly to the fourth cameraman, who said cheerily, 'Ready when you are, Mr DeMille!'

FOUL LANGUAGE

DeMille had to direct an actor, who was playing a cowboy, to fall off a horse after a rifle shot had been fired. It was a difficult scene to get right, so DeMille ordered his cameraman to keep on filming no matter what happened.

'You aren't to stop for anything,' he directed. Subsequently, the scene got under way. However, when the actor fell off his horse, the on-set doctor, thinking that the man had done himself a terrible injury, rushed up to him to provide some first aid. DeMille, infuriated by the doctor's appearance on film, jumped up from where he was sitting and, swearing at the top of his voice, ran after the doctor and chased him off set. Later that day, when everyone was sitting watching the rushes, DeMille was rather surprised to see not only the doctor dashing up to the actor, but also a bald man in hot pursuit.

'Who's that?' demanded DeMille.

'That's the studio doctor,' replied an assistant.

'Not him. I meant the other man. The one using all that disgusting language.'

'That's you, sir,' said the assistant.

'It most certainly isn't,' roared DeMille. 'It may appear to be me. It might even look like me, but I can assure you I never use foul language like that!'

BRIDAL WHERE

Two men, one young and one old, are pushing trolleys around a supermarket when they bump into one another. The old guy says to the young guy, 'Sorry about that. I'm looking for my wife, and I guess I wasn't paying attention to where I was going.' The young man says, 'That's OK. What a coincidence! I'm looking for my wife, too. I can't find her anywhere and I'm getting desperate.' The old man replies, 'Well, maybe we can help each other. What does your wife look like?' The young man says, 'Well, she is twenty-six years old, with blonde hair, blue eyes, slim, busty and she's wearing a tight black mini-skirt. What does your wife look like?' The old man says, 'Doesn't matter, son . . . let's look for yours first.'

CHILD'S PLAY

An old couple who had been married for fifty years decided to take a second honeymoon. They went to the same town, rented the same room, ate in the same restaurant and then got ready for bed. The husband noticed that his wife took a pill one hour before bed. When he asked why she did so, his wife replied that it was to make her feel younger. The husband greedily swallowed the rest of the pills. In the morning, the wife noticed that her husband was not in the room. She went to the lobby and then out in the street, where she found him sitting on the pavement. When she asked what he was doing, he replied, 'Waiting for the school bus.'

AURAL EVIDENCE

A partially deaf magistrate had just heard a case of larceny to which the defendant had pleaded guilty. The prosecutor read out a lengthy list of previous convictions for dishonesty, assault and resisting arrest. The magistrate then asked the defendant if he had anything to say in extenuation, to which the defendant replied, 'Bugger all.'

The magistrate leaned over the bench and whispered to the clerk of sessions, sitting immediately below, 'What did he say?'

The clerk replied, 'Bugger all.' The magistrate answered, 'That's funny, I could have sworn I saw his lips move.'

THE HEART OF THE MATTER

An elderly gentleman went to his doctor complaining of heart pains, but when he came out of the doctor's office, he looked worse than when he'd gone in. His wife, who was sitting in the waiting room, asked him what was wrong.

'The doctor says I have a cute vagina,' the old man whispered, ashen-faced.

'Don't be silly, dear,' his wife replied in exasperation. 'You have acute angina.'

LITTLE DONATIONS

A happily married couple with both partners in their mid-seventies were visiting a hospital one day when they passed a sign saying 'Donate To The Sperm Bank'.

The wife turned to her husband and said, 'Why don't you donate some of your sperm, dear?'

'It's no good,' replied her husband, 'I'm seventy-five years old. They're not going to want me.'

'Well, you were all right on my birthday. Go on, go and have a try.'

So the old man found a nurse and said, 'I've come to see if I can donate some of my sperm.'

The nurse was more than a little shocked, but after having asked how old he was and if he was in good health, she decided that he was a suitable candidate. Giving him a small jar with a screw-top lid, she sent him into a cubicle and told him that she would be back in half an hour to check that everything was okay.

Half an hour passed and the nurse returned to the cubicle.

'How's it going in there?' she asked.

'To be honest,' the man replied, 'I'm having a few problems. I've tried using my right hand because it is the strongest and I've tried using my left hand. I've tried putting it under the hot tap and even under the cold tap, but I still can't get the lid off this blasted jar!'

MIAOW!

Every Sunday, a sweet little old lady went to her local church and placed £200 in the collection box. This carried on for months until one day the priest approached his parishioner and said, 'Excuse me, I couldn't help but notice that every Sunday you put £200 in our collection box.'

'Oh yes,' the little old lady replied blithely, 'my son lives over in America and sends me an awful lot of money every week, so what I don't need for myself, I give to the church.'

'But how much does he send you?' said the priest. 'Because £200 is an awful lot of money.'

'He gives me £1,000 per week,' she replied proudly.

'Your son must be very successful then. What does he do?'

'He's a vet.'

'What a good profession,' sighed the priest. 'Where is it he practises?'

'Oh well, he has one cat house in Kansas and the other in Vegas,' she replied cheerfully.

PRAISE INDEED

DeMille was not the only movie mogul to suffer from the odd senior moment. Producer Samuel Goldwyn was filming one day when someone on set is said to have told him that one of his productions was magnificent.

'Magnificent,' Goldwyn was said to have snapped. 'It's more than magnificent – it's MEDIOCRE!'

STOP PRESS

An article published about Sir Francis Chichester featured a photograph of the great man alongside the following caption: 'Sir Francis Chichester – the great yachtsman who, with his 24-foot cutter, circumcised the world.'

REMEMBER TO KEEP YOUR HEAD DOWN

Hector Hugh Munro is best known by his pen name, Saki, under which he wrote numerous short stories, which were later collected into several volumes of fiction. Serving as a soldier in World War I, Saki experienced a fatal senior moment when, on reprimanding a soldier for lighting up a cigarette in the trenches, he momentarily forgot where he was and stood up – only for a German sniper to shoot him dead.

WILL YOU MARRY ME?

Two elderly people were living in a mobile-home park. He was a widower and she was a widow. They had known each other for several years when, one evening at a community supper, he leant across the table and plucked up the courage to ask her, 'Will you marry me?'

After about ten seconds of careful consideration, the old woman replied, 'Yes, yes, I'd love to marry you.'

The meal ended and, with a few pleasant exchanges, the couple went home to their respective caravans. Next morning, however, the old man couldn't remember whether the love of his life had said yes or no to his proposal. Try as he would, he just couldn't recall what she had said. With trepidation he went to the telephone and called her up. Firstly, he explained that his memory wasn't as good as it had been, but then he said what a lovely evening he'd had.

As the old man gained a little more confidence, he finally enquired, 'When I asked if you would marry me, did you say yes or no?'

He was delighted when the response came: 'Why, I said yes, I will. But I'm so glad you rang because I couldn't remember for the life of me who had asked me.'

YOU WIN SOME, YOU LOSE SOME

Wouldn't you know it – you go for years as one of Hollywood's best loved and most talented actresses, hardly ever forgetting a line, always turning up on time for your job, then you go and get nominated for an Oscar and suddenly you suffer your first senior moment! This is exactly what happened to Meryl Streep who, in 1979, was nominated for and won the Oscar for Best Supporting Actress for her role in *Kramer versus Kramer*, in which she played the estranged wife of Dustin Hoffman.

However, at the post-award festivities, Streep managed to lose her Oscar by leaving it behind in the ladies' toilets. Luckily, no other actresses walked off with the statuette and it was later returned to its rightful owner.

CHRISTMAS SPIRIT

Poet William Butler Yeats was well known for being extremely absent-minded. Towards the end of December 1913, while staying at a cottage in Sussex, he went out for a walk to the village post office, only to find on his arrival that the place was shut.

On his return home, he took out his anger on the housekeeper, who asked incredulously, 'But Mr Yeats, don't you know it's Christmas Day?'

SECOND YOUTH

'One starts to get young at the age of sixty, and then it's too late.'
— PABLO PICASSO, ARTIST

UPS AND DOWNS

A well-known supermarket chain recently upgraded one of its stores by putting in a state-of-the-art escalator on which it was possible to take specially designed shopping trolleys owing to a magnetic strip which keeps the trolleys in place. Despite numerous signs at the top and bottom of each escalator warning that a magnetic device was in operation, one particular gentleman decided to use the escalator, regardless of the unfortunate fact that he had a false leg made out of metal. Jumping on proved easy enough, but when it was time to jump off, the manoeuvre wasn't so easy, as his false leg was stuck to the magnet. Eventually, supermarket staff had to turn the escalator off in order to set the man free!

MISSION ABORTED

Two rather senile members of parliament were chatting in the tea rooms of the House of Commons one day when one turned to the other and said: 'I'm not sure what to do about the damned Abortion Bill. What do you think I should do about it, Charles?'

'Oh, if I were you, I'd pay it straight away before somebody finds out and leaks it to the press,' Charles replied.

CANINE CONFUSION

Police in Manchester were amused when a young woman came into their police station to report her dog, a toy poodle, missing. The young lady was in great distress. She told them that she had left her dog tied up outside a supermarket while she popped in to buy a magazine, only to discover when she came out that the dog had disappeared.

'There wasn't another dog outside by any chance, was there?' the policeman on the front desk asked. 'A Yorkshire terrier?'

'Yes,' said the woman. 'There were a few dogs tied up outside. I think there was a Yorkshire terrier. But Bertie is a poodle – a little black poodle.'

'We know,' said the policeman, before leading the young lady into the waiting room, where, seated in a corner, was a little old lady holding Bertie on the end of a lead.

'This is Mrs Parter,' said the policeman. 'She has just reported that she finds herself the victim of a practical joke. She went to the supermarket with her Yorkshire terrier, Angel, finished her shopping and picked Angel up on the way out. Only trouble was that when she got to the corner of the road, she met a friend who asked her if she'd got a new puppy. When Mrs Parter looked down, she was horrified to discover that someone had swapped her Angel for some scruffy little poodle!'

Angel was later recovered from outside the supermarket and reunited with her rather forgetful and myopic owner.

OLD SPORT

Two old dears were sitting on a park bench outside the local town hall in which a flower show was in progress. One leaned over and said, 'Life is so dull. We never have fun any more. If you gave me a fiver, I'd take my clothes off and streak through that flower show!'

'You're on!' said her friend, holding up a crisp five-pound note. As fast as she could, the first old lady fumbled her way out of her clothes and, stark naked, streaked through the front door of the flower show.

Waiting outside, her friend soon heard a huge commotion inside the hall, followed by loud and raucous applause. The naked lady burst out through the door surrounded by a cheering crowd.

'What happened?' asked her waiting friend.

'I won first prize as Best Dried Arrangement!'

DRESS SENSE

Mary's mother-in-law was always dropping by her house unexpectedly and, on one particular afternoon, she did as she always did, and knocked on her daughter-in-law's door. But when the door opened, to her amazement, Mary was stark naked.

'What on earth are you up to?' she asked.

'What do you think? I'm waiting for your gorgeous son to come home from the office.'

'But you're stark naked!'

'This is my love dress,' said Mary, proudly.

'But it's not a dress, you're naked.'

'Your son loves me wearing this dress. In fact, it's his favourite dress in my whole wardrobe. It makes him so happy when I wear it. But you're going to have to go now, he'll be home soon and he won't appreciate it as much if you're here.'

By this time, Mary's mother-in-law had heard quite enough so she left, but all the way home she thought about what her daughter-in-law had said and about how happy the love dress made her son, so when she got back to her own house she took a bath and then waited, naked, by her front door.

When her husband got home he walked into the hallway, only to see his wife standing naked by the hatstand.

'What on earth are you doing?' he asked.

'I'm wearing my love dress,' his wife replied, as sexily as she was able.

'Needs ironing,' he growled.

THEATRICAL SPECTACLE

One evening, an elderly, bespectacled gentleman went to the opera. Before going into the auditorium, he went to the bar to order some champagne. But just before going to find his seat, he heard an announcement over the theatre's loudspeakers warning that 'All glasses must be left at the bar.' Never one to ignore the rules, the old man removed his glasses and spent the rest of the evening wondering what on earth was happening on stage.

'I just don't think of age and time in respect of years. I have too much experience of people in their seventies who are vigorous and useful and people who are thirty-five who are in lousy physical shape and can't think straight. I don't think age has that much to do with it.'
— HARRISON FORD, ACTOR

QUEEN VICTORIA

Short-sightedness can often contribute to senior moments, as the following anecdote perfectly illustrates. According to Robert Rhodes James in his book *Rosebery*, Lord Portarlington once approached Queen Victoria, saying, 'I know your face quite well, but damn it, I cannot put a name to it!'

MAGGIE'S MISTAKE

In 1985, Margaret Thatcher was addressing guests gathered at a reception in Jakarta, Indonesia. 'We are all impressed by the way that President Suharto and his Cabinet are handling the problems of Malaysia.' The Prime Minister's husband, Denis, whispered in his wife's ear, 'Indonesia, dear, not Malaysia.' Correcting herself, Thatcher thanked her husband before resuming her speech.

IGNOMINIOUS DEATH

One day, a doctor had to be the bearer of bad news, when he informed a woman that her husband had died of a massive myocardial infarct. Not much more than five minutes later, the doctor overheard her reporting to the rest of her family that her husband had died of a 'massive internal fart'.

THE ABSENT-MINDED PROFESSOR

On one occasion, the Oxford Library Club had booked a guest speaker to lecture them on the subject of 'Old Age, Absent-Mindedness and Keeping Fit' and all its members were greatly looking forward to hearing the speech . . . unfortunately, the event was somewhat marred by the fact that the doctor forgot to turn up.

DRIVING IN THE DARK

Driving can precipitate some of the worst senior moments ever experienced, not least because you are in control of a lethal weapon. This alarming phenomenon has never been more clearly demonstrated than by Rosemary Parr from Falmouth in Cornwall when she was given a hire car while her own vehicle was in the garage for its annual MOT.

Picking up the new smart car, Rosemary quite happily drove off to work. In her lunch hour she drove to the shops to collect some groceries, then drove back to work for the afternoon. But when it came to driving home later that day, she couldn't understand why she was finding it so difficult to see far in front of her. Suddenly it struck her . . . she hadn't switched her headlights on . . . and she had no idea which switch to turn to make them come on! Frantically, she tried several buttons and knobs, but nothing seemed to work; very gingerly, she travelled the rest of the way home in the dark, all the time trying to work out which switch might throw a little more light on the subject.

Just as Rosemary was pulling into her driveway, she located the right button. And then there was light. Relieved that she'd made it all the way home without causing an accident, she went to bed with a cup of cocoa. It was only when she got up the next morning and got into her car to drive to work that she realized her second fatal mistake. The car wouldn't start. No matter what she did, nothing worked . . . then suddenly the penny dropped. Having found out where the lights were the previous evening, she'd forgotten to turn them off! The car battery was as dead as a dodo.

HYPOCHONDRIAC HAPPENINGS

The older we get, the more we start to suffer from various ailments. However, some people can take the idea of looking out for symptoms just a little too far, as the following joke perfectly illustrates.

Mr Frank was an acute hypochondriac and should never have attended the medical lecture on diseases of the kidney, but unfortunately he did, and the very next day he called on his doctor. The doctor attempted to explain that in that particular disease there was no pain or discomfort of any kind.

'I knew it,' gasped Mr Frank, fretfully. 'My symptoms exactly.'

E. M. FORSTER

According to Kenneth Rose in *Kings, Queens and Courtiers*, the novelist E. M. Forster once bowed to a wedding cake when attending the wedding reception of Lord Harewood. It seems that Forster had mistaken the gastronomic creation for Queen Mary.

FENCED IN

Nicola, in her mid-forties, had always enjoyed keeping as physically fit as possible. She went for long walks regularly, went to the gym three times a week and practised yoga in her spare time. In addition to all this, Nicola recently decided that she wanted to take up fencing again. Spotting an advert in the local newspaper for fencing lessons, she eagerly rang the number supplied and asked the gentleman on the other end of the line what kind of fencing he taught.

'I don't understand, what do you mean by what kind of fencing?'

'Well,' replied Nicola, 'is it épée or sabre? I can fence to gold standard in épée, but I'd be quite happy to learn sabre.'

There was a long silence.

'OK,' said the man, 'but all I teach is the old-fashioned type of fencing – you know, the sort with posts and wire?'

Consumed by embarrassment, Nicola hung up the phone.

Now, this story would not be quite so bad if, one year later, on seeing the same advert for fencing classes, Nicola hadn't picked up the phone and made the same mistake all over again.

FALLING APART

'Just when I finally got my head together,
my body fell apart.'

– ANON.

CHICKEN TONIGHT

An elderly gentleman decided that his wife was getting a little hard of hearing, so he called her doctor to make an appointment to have her hearing checked. The doctor said he could see her in two weeks, but that in the meantime there was a simple, informal test which the husband could do to give the doctor some idea of the gravity of the problem.

'Here's what you do. Start about 40 feet away from her, and speak in a normal conversational tone, and see if she hears you. If not, go to 30 feet, then 20 feet, and so on until you get a response.'

So that same evening, when the man's wife was in the kitchen cooking dinner, and he was in the living room, he stationed himself about 40 feet away and decided to see what happened.

'Darling, what's for dinner?'

No reply.

Moving into the dining room, about 20 feet away, he again asked, 'Honey, what's for dinner?'

Again, there came no response from his wife.

The man approached the kitchen door, so that he was only 10 feet away. 'Sweetheart, what's for dinner?'

Silence.

The man walked right up behind his wife and asked, 'Dearest, what's for dinner?'

'For the fourth time,' his wife yelled back, 'chicken!'

CHRONIC CASES

A man going through an Iowa courthouse metal detector emptied his pockets into the security tray, only to realize when it was too late that he had placed a large packet of marijuana in the tray alongside everything else.

When the man realized his mistake, he tried to make a quick getaway, but luck was not on his side as he ran in the wrong direction straight into a locked revolving door.

'He threw in a baggie of marijuana without realizing it, and the person working the security post said, "Hey, what's this?"' said the Iowa chief deputy. 'He kind of gave that old "I've-been-caught" look, and the chase was on.'

Along the same lines, in September 2002, a customer at a Kentucky Fried Chicken outlet in California was surprised to discover that, along with his order of chicken, he was also served two bags of marijuana. The man serving him was clearly suffering a severe senior moment when he'd placed the bags of marijuana on the man's tray.

The customer politely handed the bags back, then called the police. 'Authorities believe [the KFC employee] was selling marijuana to customers who used a secret word as a code,' said a Marin County Sheriff's spokesman.

SHORT-TERM MEMORY

Two old friends are talking and one says to the other, 'Did you know that the second thing to go is your memory?' His friend asks, 'What's the first?' 'I can't remember.'

APPROACHING SIXTY

'With sixty staring me in the face, I have developed
inflammation of the sentence structure and a definite
hardening of the paragraphs.'

— JAMES THURBER, WRITER

GRAVESIDE HUMOUR

Not every senior moment need be funny – in fact there are plenty
which are more like moments of clarification and enlightenment;
such is the case of Robert Wilton, the English comedian, who was
attending the funeral of a close friend one day. Already quite old
himself, at the end of the service Wilton was heard to say: 'There's
not much point going home really, is there?'

WOMEN'S TROUBLES

In March 2001, Jeanie Linders's new musical premiered in
Orlando, Florida. Described by one reviewer as a 'hilarious
celebration of women and The Change, this original parody
chronicles the meeting of four women at a lingerie sale at
Bloomingdale's with nothing in common but a black lace bra
. . . and memory loss, hot flashes, night sweats, hormones,
not enough sex and more.' The show's title? *Menopause – The
Musical*.

TAXI SERVICE

One evening, a police car pulled up in front of an old woman's house and the woman's elderly husband climbed out. The policeman explained to his wife that her husband had told them that he was lost in the neighbourhood park and couldn't find his way home.

'Oh, Jim,' said the old woman. 'You've been going to that park for over thirty years! How could you get lost?'

Leaning close to his wife, so that the policeman couldn't hear, the old man whispered, 'I wasn't lost. I was just too tired to walk home.'

DOCTOR'S ORDERS

An old man goes to the doctor and tells him that he hasn't been feeling well. The doctor examines him, leaves the room, and comes back with three different bottles of pills.

The doctor says, 'Take the blue pill with a big glass of water when you get up. Take the green pill with a big glass of water after lunch. Then, before going to bed, take the red pill with another big glass of water.'

Startled to be put on so much medication, the elderly man stammers, 'Exactly what is my problem? Tell me, is it serious?'

'You're not drinking enough water.'

PLANE MAD

On a transatlantic flight, an elderly passenger kept peering out the window. Since it was completely dark outside, all she could see was the blinking wing-tip light. Finally, she rang for the flight attendant.

'I'm sorry to bother you,' she said, 'but I think you should inform the pilot that his left indicator is on and has been for some time . . .'

HOW TO CATCH A CRIMINAL

As we have already discovered, thieves are often guilty of more than just robbery; they are also some of the worst culprits when it comes to senior moments, as the following story illustrates.

A young woman reported her car stolen and mentioned that there was a car phone in it. The policeman taking the report called the phone and told the person who answered that he had seen an advertisement in the newspaper and wanted to buy the car. They arranged to meet, and the thief was arrested.

TOILET HUMOUR

A confused and disorientated man walks into a Catholic church, sits down in the confessional box and says nothing. The bewildered priest coughs to attract his attention, but still the man says nothing. The priest then knocks on the wall three times in a final attempt to get the man to speak. Finally, the man replies, 'No use knocking, mate – there's no paper in this one either.'

ANCIENT ADONIS

A sixty-year-old man visited his doctor for a check-up. The doctor told him, 'You're in terrific shape. There's nothing wrong with you. You might even live forever; you have the fitness levels of a thirty-year-old. By the way, how old was your father when he died?'

'Who said he was dead?'

The doctor was surprised and asked, 'How old is he and is he very active?'

'Well, he is eighty years old and he still goes to the gym three times a week and plays tennis and badminton regularly.'

The doctor was astounded at this information and asked, 'Well, how old was your grandfather when he died?'

'Who said he was dead?'

The doctor was astonished. He said, 'You mean to tell me you are sixty years old and both your father and your grandfather are alive? Is your grandfather active?'

'He goes skiing at least once a season and is a regular at his local pool. Not only that,' added the patient boastfully, 'my grandfather is 104 years old, and next week he is getting married again.'

The doctor said, 'Why on earth would your grandfather want to get married at his age?'

'Who said he wanted to?'

BLIND PANIC

Opticians are no doubt used to checking out elderly people's eyesight, but nothing prepared Hayley Tomalain for the following incident, which occurred at her clinic in June 1997. Hayley asked her client to stand twenty feet away from the eyesight chart, cover his left eye with one hand and read the letters. The client did this perfectly and Hayley then asked him to cover his right eye with one hand and repeat the exercise. Again the client read the chart from top to bottom without any problem.

'Now try it with both,' said Hayley. To her surprise, the client could read nothing at all, not even the letters in large print. Turning around to see what the matter was, the optician saw that her client had covered both eyes with his hands and was saying, 'Nope, I can't see a thing!'

HAVE YOU A SCREW LOOSE?

In 1985 in Cannes, South of France, it was reported that doctors at a major hospital were baffled when, after a routine X-ray was carried out on a man who had complained of severe headaches, they found what looked like a 7-inch screwdriver embedded in the man's skull.

On closer inspection, it was discovered that the screwdriver was not, thankfully, in the man's head, but in the X-ray machine itself, where a somewhat forgetful technician had left it.

AGE-DEFYING MOMENT

'Now, Ms Lyons,' said the doctor, 'you say you have shooting pains in your neck, dizziness and constant nausea. Just for the record, how old are you?'

'Why, I'm going to be thirty-nine on my next birthday,' the woman replied indignantly.

'Hmmm,' muttered the doctor, 'got a slight case of memory loss, too.'

IDENTITY CRISIS

One of the many funny stories told about President George Bush concerns a visit he once made to an old people's home. After speaking to a few of the residents, the president asked of one old lady, 'Do you know who I am?'

'No,' came the snappy reply, 'but I'm sure if you ask at reception they'll be able to tell you.'

YOUNG AT HEART
'He says he's young at heart – but slightly older
in other places.'
– ANON.

AGEING WELL?

We all know how rude it is to ask a person's age and we all know how humiliating it is when you tell someone how old you are, only for them to smile wanly as if to say: '*Only* thirty-five? I thought you were at least forty.' So imagine the English music-hall comedian Wee Georgie Wood's reaction when, on hopping into a taxi and telling the driver to take him to the British Museum, the driver turned round and said: 'You're taking a bloody chance, aren't you?'

WHO AM I?

As well as being absent-minded, Tennyson's father – the Reverend George Clayton Tennyson – was also said to be rather forgetful. On visiting one of his elderly parishioners, he was greeted at the door by a maid.

'And whom shall I say is calling?' the maid asked politely, at which point Tennyson's mind went blank. For the life of him, he couldn't remember his name. Several seconds passed, after which the reverend decided to call it a day and go home. As he turned around and headed down the path, a tradesman passed him and, raising his hat, greeted the old man.

'Good day to you, Dr Tennyson,' the tradesman said.

'By God, my man, you're absolutely right,' replied the reverend, who afterwards returned to his duties and went to meet his elderly parishioner.

GET ME TO THE CHURCH ON TIME

With the invention of the digital camera, the days when you took hundreds of precious holiday snaps or baby photos only to realize that you hadn't put any film in the damn camera are long gone. But for one wedding photographer, a man by the name of Frank Esquival, this was no compensation when it was time to photograph a friend's special day. Having been booked at least four months in advance to take photographs for his oldest friend's wedding, he turned up half an hour early to set up all his equipment and to check out the best possible backgrounds for the formal photographs after the service.

When it was time for the wedding party to arrive, imagine Esquival's horror when, instead of a Bentley decorated with white ribbons pulling up at the gates, a hearse arrived instead! Frank, in what can only be described as a classic senior moment, had got the wrong church, and although he rushed to get to the right one in time, he arrived just as the disgruntled couple were driving away!

CROAK, FROG, CROAK

A grandfather and his grandson were walking in the woods and came to a small pond. The grandfather asked, 'Did you hear that frog croak?' The grandson replied that he did and asked, 'Can you croak?' The grandfather didn't pay any attention until he heard another frog and again asked the grandson if he could hear the frog croak. And again, the grandson asked if he could croak. The grandfather then asked, 'Why do you keep asking me if I can croak?' His grandson promptly replied, 'Dad told me that when you croak, we'll get a lot of money.'

PUZZLED POET

As well as being Poet Laureate and penning such famous works as 'The Lady of Shalott' and 'Maud', Alfred, Lord Tennyson was also noted for his absent-mindedness.

Lunching one day with a group of friends and his wife, Tennyson was heard to ask of one particular gentleman: 'Do you know anything about the poet Lovell?'

'Why, my dear,' interjected Mrs Tennyson, 'this is Mr Lovell.'

RIPE OLD AGE

'At my age I don't even buy green bananas.'
– GEORGE BURNS, COMEDIAN

JUST THE TICKET

Justice Oliver Wendell Holmes Junior once boarded a train in Washington DC and settled himself into his seat. However, when the ticket collector approached,  Holmes was unable to find his ticket. Luckily, the conductor recognized his distinguished passenger and said, 'Never mind, sir, I'm sure that when you come across it you will be good enough to send it into us at head office.'

Justice Oliver Wendell Holmes Junior was, however, not so concerned about the railway company, as about another far more pressing concern.

'Never mind sending the ticket to head office,' he said. 'What's worrying me is how I'm supposed to know where to get off without it.'

WRONG SIDE OF THE BED

Sometimes, no matter how well one looks after oneself, and no matter how much exercise one takes, there's no escaping a senior moment. Such was the case for actor Peter O'Toole who, at seventy-four, is still a sprightly young thing. Nevertheless, when his physiotherapist said he should start taking gentle exercise,

O'Toole went along to the cricket school at Lords and spent six weeks there, saying afterwards: 'I confess that I felt very good indeed. Come Christmas, I woke up and thought, "I'm awake and I don't have to work. How lovely!" I jumped out of bed, tripped on a pair of shoes and busted my hip. How's that for being fit?'

ROOM SERVICE

As we know only too well, deafness is one of the many signs of ageing and is moreover the source of many a senior moment – as infamous British chef and enfant terrible of the culinary world, Marco Pierre White, discovered to his cost.

According to an article in *The Guardian*, the celebrity chef, who was in America to publicize his autobiography, *White Slave*, was relaxing in his hotel room when he heard a knock on the door. 'It was a room-service man outside, who kept repeating that he had brought three hookers for me,' said White, who then went on to explain that he thought the prostitutes must have been sent by one of his friends to help cheer him up after a rather public spat he'd had with his wife back in London. However, when White opened the door, what he found was not quite what he'd imagined, for the hotel employee was carrying a dish of three complimentary cookies. 'I was surprised rather than disappointed,' said White, who no doubt then went to the bathroom to clean out his ears.

LAST REQUEST

An elderly man named Morris returns home from his doctor's appointment and tells his wife that the doctor has told him he has only twenty-four hours left to live. Given the prognosis, Morris asks his wife for sex. Naturally, his wife agrees to the proposition and they make love. Six hours later, he again approaches his wife and says, 'Sweetheart, you know that I now have only eighteen hours to live. Could we please do it again? Of course, his wife again agrees and they make love for the second time. Later, as Morris climbs into bed, he looks at his watch and realizes that he now has only eight hours left to live. He touches his wife's shoulder and asks, 'Honey, please, just one more time before I die.' She says, 'Of course, darling,' and they make love for a third time. After this session, his wife rolls over and falls asleep. Morris, however, anxious about his impending death, tosses and turns and cannot sleep. The next time he checks his watch, he has only four hours left to live. He taps his wife on the shoulder and she wakes up. 'Darling,' he begins, 'I only have another four hours. Do you think we could . . .' At this point, his wife sits up straight and says, 'Listen, Morris, I have to get up in the morning . . . you don't.'

LOST PROPERTY

Ever gone into a petrol station, filled up your car with fuel, paid at the counter and driven away, only to realize you've forgotten something and had to turn back? This is precisely what happened to a Macedonian man who, in 2006, was travelling through Italy with his wife and daughter. Stopping at an Italian service station, the man filled up his car with petrol, then went and paid at the desk, after which he got back into the car and headed for Milan. It was only when he was 340km away that he realized something wasn't right. Suddenly the penny dropped; his wife wasn't in the car.

The woman, who was from Georgia, had gone to the lavatory, only to return to the petrol-station forecourt to find her husband had driven off without her. Unable to speak a word of Italian, and with no official documents on her person, it took her well over an hour to communicate to police what had happened.

Her husband later explained his error by saying that his wife usually travelled in the back of the car with his daughter and therefore it wasn't until he asked her a question and she didn't answer that he realized something was wrong.

As senior moments go, surely this must rate as one of the stupidest?

SECOND INFANCY

Two elderly gentlemen from a retirement home were sitting on a park bench under a large sycamore tree when one turned to the other and said: 'John, I'm eighty-three years old now and I'm just full of aches and pains. I know you're about my age. How do you feel?'

John replied, 'I feel like a newborn baby.'

'Really? Like a newborn baby?'

'Yep – no hair, no teeth and I think I just wet my pants.'

HAIR TODAY, GONE TOMORROW

A hairdressing salon in Los Angeles was sued in May 2005 when one of its staff suffered a truly awful senior moment. The unfortunate member of staff, having applied a perm solution to the hair of one of her customers, went to take a phone call from her boyfriend. By the time the stylist got back to work, the customer was complaining of an unpleasant burning sensation to her scalp, not to mention a severe headache. Realizing that she had left the perming solution on for far too long, the hair stylist immediately tried to wash her customer's head, but it was too late. The woman's scalp was severely damaged and all her hair had fallen out. Ouch!

STEAMY ANTICS

In 2006, a woman from Wiltshire, England, was woken up by what she thought was an obscene phone call. Someone was heavy breathing and groaning down the phone at her. The woman paid the call no attention, but when the phone rang for a second time she thought she recognized her daughter's voice.

'Oh my God,' her daughter was saying, after which there was the distinct sound of a man's voice.

Ringing the police, the woman described the two phone calls and said she thought her daughter, who lived approximately one hundred miles away, was being attacked.

The police rushed round to the daughter's house, only to be met by the bewildered young woman and her partner, who explained that they had been enjoying a steamy moment of passion and must have pushed the automatic speed-dial on their telephone.

ELEPHANTS NEVER FORGET

Elephants never forget? Good for them, they've obviously never been faced with anything more complicated than remembering not to sit on a fence. For those of us who don't sport jazzy grey trunks, however, life isn't quite so simple. Each day it seems we are faced with a gamut of new, insurmountable challenges, such as remembering if we swallowed the pill which we now can't locate.

A few years ago in December, an elderly lady by the name of Caroline attended her grandson's birthday party. The festivities occurred at lunchtime, during which the adults present consumed more than a few glasses of wine. Afterwards, Caroline decided on a spot of shopping. Bidding her family goodbye, she left the party and walked down towards the centre of town, during which time it dawned on her that several passers-by were looking at her quite strangely. Having consumed a few beverages and being in an extremely festive spirit, she ignored the odd looks and continued merrily on her way until, having stopped in front of a shop window, she glanced first downwards and then very slowly upwards, only to be met by a terrifying reflection in the glass.

To her horror, Caroline now realized why everyone had been staring at her. A crumpled pink party hat sat on her head, whilst draped around her shoulders were the remnants of the multicoloured party string with which her grandchildren had covered her.

UTTER BALDERDASH!

Softening of the brain is often attributed to senior momentitus – that moment when words fail you, when nothing makes sense, when the more you try to explain something, the more befuddled your explanation becomes. Take, for instance, the following extract from a letter, which was sent to R. F. Mould by a sales manager:

> I fully realize that I have not succeeded in answering all of your questions . . . Indeed, I feel I have not answered any of them completely. The answers I have found only serve to raise a whole new set of questions, which only lead to more problems, some of which we weren't even aware were problems. To sum it up . . . in some ways I feel we are as confused as ever, but I believe we are confused on a higher level, and about more important things.

WORDS OF WISDOM

'But I'll tell you the really great thing about living to be ninety-three: one does not have any rivals because they're all dead, so one can afford to be generous with young chaps like you.'
— BEN TRAVERS, WRITER

SLOW COACH

Have you ever wondered what would happen to you if you were too slow crossing a road? You might think that you were likely to get knocked down by a passing car or that some irate driver might sound his horn at you. Imagine one elderly woman's surprise when a motorcycle cop gave her a ticket for crossing the road too slowly!

'I think it's completely outrageous. He treated me like a six-year-old, like I don't know what I'm doing,' said eighty-two-year-old Mayvis Coyle unhappily.

A spokesperson for the Los Angeles Valley Traffic Division explained in response that the police were trying to cut down on pedestrian accidents.

But that is little comfort to poor Mayvis Coyle.

TEETHING PROBLEMS

Waiter: Would you like an aperitif, sir?
Customer: No, thank you. I always use my own dentures.

BIRTH CONTROL

An elderly woman went into the doctor's office. When the doctor asked why she was there, she replied, 'I'd like to have some birth-control pills.' Taken aback, the doctor thought for a minute and then said, 'Excuse me, Mrs White, but you are seventy-five years old. What possible use could you have for birth-control pills?' The woman responded, 'They help me sleep better.' The doctor thought some more and continued, 'How in the world do birth-control pills help you to sleep?' The woman answered, 'I put them in my granddaughter's orange juice and I sleep better at night.'

'MY WHOLE CORPUS' AND OTHER WORKS

Sometimes it is difficult to discern the difference between a senior moment and sheer stupidity. Such is the case with the following anecdote, which involves the poet and critic T. S. Eliot.

Whilst travelling around America in 1948, Eliot was awarded the Nobel Prize for Literature by the Swedes. An eager young reporter asked him if he had been given the prize for 'The Waste Land'. Eliot, polite as ever, replied that no, he had been given the award for his whole corpus.

When the article appeared the following day, Eliot was somewhat bemused to read that, 'In an interview with our airport correspondent this morning, Mr Eliot revealed that the Swedish Academy had given him the Nobel Prize not for "The Waste Land", but for his poem "My Whole Corpus".'

LANGUAGE BARRIER

A bilingual man went off to work in France. His elderly mother was anxious as she was used to speaking to him every day, but he reassured her that she could phone as often as she wanted.

Time passed after he'd arrived, however, and she didn't call once. Was it the cost? Had she lost the number? Concerned, he rang to find out.

'I tried to call you four times!' she said angrily. 'Each time, a rude Frenchman spoke over the top of me. He made no attempt to listen to me or to fetch you. I don't want to talk to him again.'

The penny dropped. The old lady had been speaking to his answerphone message.

KNOCK, KNOCK, WHO'S THERE?

When Clara Thomson's eighteen-year-old daughter, Milly, came home in tears one day, saying that someone had bumped into her new car and that it was scratched down the whole of one side, Mrs Thomson was understandably upset. But when Milly also told her mother that the person responsible was a young woman who lived a few blocks away and that she'd been incredibly rude to her, Mrs Thomson decided to take matters into her own hands. Storming out of the house, she went to give the woman a piece of her mind. The only problem was that, in her haste to defend her daughter, Mrs Thomson had heard the address incorrectly. Her daughter had said Stanley Crescent, but Mrs Thomson had heard Stanley Close. Turning up at what she thought was the right door, she proceeded to give the woman who opened it a piece of her mind. It was only when Milly, who had been trying to catch her mother up, finally shouted that she'd got the wrong house, that Clara realized her embarrassing mistake.

THE MAD SCIENTIST

Even a genius is capable of – or perhaps more qualified to have – senior moments. The most famous scientist of them all, Albert Einstein, was not exempt from the odd senior moment or two. So the story goes that when Einstein departed on his second trip to the United States with his wife, Elsa, he first lost his wife, then found her, then he lost his tickets, and then found them.

CHANGE OF ADDRESS

In the 1980s, a fifty-year-old man by the name of Jermund Skogstad was busy moving into his new flat in Oslo, Norway, when he decided to get a bite to eat. When Skogstad had finished eating at a café, he reached into his pocket and discovered that he had forgotten his wallet, which contained both his money and his new address – an address he could not remember for the life of him. The Norwegian was later quoted as saying that he hoped his new landlady would read the story and inform him of the location of his new home.

FLOWER ARRANGING

Four senior women were in a beauty parlour getting their hair done when a young woman walked in, wearing a low-cut blouse that revealed a rosebud tattoo above one breast.

One lady leaned over to another and said, 'She doesn't know it yet, but in fifty years time, it'll look like a long-stemmed rose in a hanging basket.'

IT'S A MYSTERY

One of the world's most famous and best loved authors, Agatha Christie, who in her lifetime wrote a huge number of murder mysteries including *Murder on the Orient Express* and *Death on the Nile*, was herself the subject of one of the most mysterious disappearances in literary history. On 3 December 1926, Christie, having driven off from her home in Berkshire, ostensibly vanished off the face of the earth. Police, alerted to her disappearance by her husband, consequently mounted a massive search for the missing author, one that involved over 15,000 volunteers. Ten days later, she was discovered at a Yorkshire hotel and health spa, registered under another name. Christie herself claimed she had been the victim of a bout of amnesia, but it is not out of the question that what she was really suffering from was a rather prolonged senior moment.

GOLDEN OLDIES

'Mrs Brown, You've Got a Lovely Walker'
– Herman's Hermits

'How Can You Mend a Broken Hip?'
– The Bee Gees

'You Make Me Feel Like Napping'
– Leo Sayer

'I Get By With a Little Help From Depends'
– The Beatles

'The First Time Ever I Forgot Your Face'
– Roberta Flack

'I Can't See Clearly Now'
– Johnny Nash

'Fifty Ways to Lose Your Liver'
– Paul Simon

'Once, Twice, Three Times to the Bathroom'
– The Commodores

'I Heard It Through the Grape Nuts'
– Marvin Gaye

'A Whiter Shade Of Hair'
– Procol Harum

SHARE AND SHARE ALIKE

One evening, an elderly couple walked into their local branch of a fast-food chain. They looked out of place amongst all the other, much younger customers, some of whom glanced up from their hamburgers and looked on the couple admiringly. You could tell what the admirers were thinking: 'Look, there is a couple who have been through a lot together, probably for sixty years or more!'

The old man walked up to the counter, placed his order and paid for his meal. The couple took a table near a window, then started taking food off the tray.

The old man unwrapped a burger and carefully cut it in half, placing one half in front of his wife. Then he carefully counted out the fries, divided them in two piles and placed one pile in front of his wife. He took a sip of the drink, his wife took a sip and then set the container down between them.

As the man began to eat his few bites of burger, the other customers began to get restless. Again, you could tell what they were thinking: 'That poor old couple can afford only one meal between the two of them.'

As the man began to eat his fries, one young man stood up and came over to the old couple's table. He politely offered to buy another meal for the old couple to eat. The old man thanked him, but said that they were fine and that they were used to sharing everything.

Then the other customers noticed that the little old lady hadn't eaten a bite of her food. She just sat there watching her husband eat and occasionally taking turns sipping the drink. Again, the young man came over and begged them to let him buy them something to eat. This time the lady explained that no, they were used to sharing everything together.

As the little old man finished eating and was wiping his face neatly with a napkin, the young man could stand it no longer. Again, he came over to their table and offered to buy some food. After being politely refused again, he finally asked a question of the little old lady.

'Why aren't you eating? You said you share everything. What is it you are waiting for?'

She answered, 'My teeth.'

HEADLINE NEWS

No one is safe from making the occasional blunder and this includes journalists. Senior moments often creep into newspaper copy, as the following selection of quotes – all of them sent to the now defunct journal *World Medicine* – broadly illustrates.

'The hospital's new diagnostic services include three X-ray rooms and nine extra places in the mortuary.'
– *ORMSKIRK ADVERTISER*

'Lost: green silk umbrella belonging to lady with one broken rib and curiously shaped ivory head.'
– *HERTS ADVERTISER*

'Even the post-mortem failed to establish a precise diagnosis and no useful treatment was subsequently initiated.'
– HOSPITAL DOCTOR

'Two hundred and twenty-three patients have been waiting for gynaecological surgery on their ears, nose or throat.'
– *MANCHESTER EVENING NEWS*

'For Sale: Rolls Royce hearse, with 1965 body.'
– *DROITWICH GAZETTE*

'Event Nine: The Norden Trophy for the cow with the best udder. Presented by Mr Norden in memory of Mrs Norden.'
GUERNSEY AGRICULTURAL SHOW BROCHURE

'Although suicide by a shot in the neck was atypical, the experts said, there were a number of references in scientific literature which described it as a safe method.'
– *THE GUARDIAN*

'Throwing caution to the wind, I ordered a tournedos and half a giraffe of wine.'
– *MANCHESTER EVENING NEWS*

'Reminiscing about Empire Days past, she told the Policy & Resources Committee: "In the morning we saluted the flag, and in the afternoon we had it off."'
– *WORTHING GAZETTE*

'Wanted: Assistant or associate professor in plastic, reconstructive and bum surgery.'
– UNIVERSITY OF KUWAIT ADVERTISEMENT

'Members of the family request mourners to omit floral tributes. The deceased was allergic to flowers.'
– NEW YORK OBITUARY COLUMN

VANISHING ACT
'My dad's pants kept creeping up on him.
By sixty-five, he was just a pair of pants and a head.'
– JEFF ALTMAN, COMEDIAN

FERRETED OUT

A thirty-five-year-old woman named Suzi was moving house from London to Guildford. When the removal firm arrived, Suzi made the men a cup of tea and in the course of conversation asked one of them, a fifty-year-old man named Tommy, to describe the worst moment in his long career as a removal man.

Tommy thought for a while before beginning his woeful narrative. Approximately two years earlier, Tommy had been doing a job in Barnes, packing up the entire contents of a four-storey house. By the end of the day, he was exhausted, but he still had one last room to do, so wearily he put everything he could see into crates, packed them into the van and finally drove off.

Halfway across London, his mobile phone began to ring. It was the woman whose house he had been working in.

'She was screaming at me down the phone,' Tommy said. 'Apparently, I had only gone and packed up the family's pet ferret, Barney. I slammed on the brakes, parked and ran round to the back of the van. I knew exactly which crate he was in because I could hear him scrabbling about. Tearing open the lid, I withdrew his cage and then – just to make certain he hadn't suffered – I took him out of the cage, at which point Barney sunk his teeth into my hand and wouldn't let go. A passer-by had to help me unlock his jaw.

'That was definitely my worst moment; my back ached, I'd packed the family ferret in a crate and then been attacked by it so badly that I had to have five stitches put in my hand. By the end of the day, I felt I'd aged twenty years.'

TOILET TRAINING

Seventy-year-old John went for his annual physical. All of his tests came back with normal results. Dr Adams said, 'John, everything looks great physically. How are you doing mentally and spiritually? Are you at peace with yourself, and do you have a good relationship with God?'

John replied, 'God and I are close. He knows I have poor eyesight, so he has arranged that when I get up in the middle of the night to go to the bathroom the light goes on and when I'm finished the light goes off.'

'Wow!' exclaimed Dr Adams. 'That's incredible!'

A little later in the day, Dr Adams called John's wife.

'Sarah,' he said, 'John is doing fine. Physically, he's great. But I had to call because I'm in amazed by his relationship with God. Is it true that he gets up during the night and the light goes on in the bathroom and then when he is finished the light goes off?'

Sarah exclaimed, 'Oh my God! He's peeing in the refrigerator again!'

OIL'S NOT LOST

Author Joseph Conrad, whose novels include *Heart of Darkness* and *Lord Jim*, was not always lucky when it came to literary matters. Writing a serialization of one of his stories for *Blackwood's Magazine* and rushing to get it to his editors on time,

Conrad is said to have suffered a chronic senior moment when he knocked over an oil lamp on to his manuscript and destroyed everything on his desk. Confronted with few other options, Conrad had to rewrite the entire instalment.

PHILOSOPHICAL RAMBLINGS

One day, the psychologist and philosopher, William James, was walking down a street in Cambridge, Massachusetts, with a couple of his students when one pointed out a white-bearded man talking to himself. The student remarked, 'Whoever he is, he's the epitome of the absent-minded professor.' James replied swiftly, 'What you really mean is that he is present-minded somewhere else.'

HOW QUICKLY WE FORGET

Two elderly gentlemen, Roger and Ted, are sitting in rocking chairs outside their nursing home when a nice young woman walks past wearing a pink miniskirt.

Roger said, 'Ted, did you see that?'

Ted replied, 'Yes I did, Roger, lovely, wasn't she?'

Roger rocked a little faster in his chair. 'I'd like to take her out, wine her, dine her and . . . and . . . Ted, what was that other thing we used to do?'

HAPPY BIRTHDAY

When an eighty-year-old woman was asked if there were to be candles on her cake, she responded curtly, 'No, it's a birthday party, not a torchlit procession.'

FALLING ASLEEP ON THE ROB

If there were a rule book for how not to execute a robbery, then one of the tips would surely be not to go to sleep on the job. Sadly for one Texan thief, such a rule book does not exist, otherwise he would never have been arrested.

Early one morning, an employee at a large department store

arrived for work to discover that the shop had been ransacked. Checking upstairs to see if any damage had occurred there, the shop assistant found that the toilet had been used but not flushed and that sitting to one side of a washbasin was a large handgun. On venturing next door, the employee came across the burglar fast asleep in a bed.

'He was disorientated and said he was sleeping and wanted to be left alone,' said the officer who later arrested the man who had fallen asleep on the rob.

PAINFUL LABOUR

One day, a man rushed into the busy Accident & Emergency department of a London hospital and shouted to the receptionist that his wife was just about to give birth in a taxi. Picking up his bag of instruments, one of the junior doctors ran out to the taxi, jumped inside, lifted up the woman's dress and told her to remove her underwear. It was only when the doctor saw the horrified expression on the woman's face that he realized his horrendous mistake. The taxi he was in was one of several outside the hospital and he had jumped, unwittingly, into the wrong one.

'My fifty years have shown me that few people know what they are talking about. I don't mean idiots who don't know. I mean everyone.'
– JOHN CLEESE, ACTOR AND COMEDIAN

POPPING THE QUESTION

An elderly man asked his wife of fifty years, 'If you had to do it over again, would you marry me?'

'You've asked me that before,' she answered.

'What did you reply?'

'I don't remember.'

HOLY SMOKE

As far as visits to the Vatican go, the one that President Richard Nixon made to the Pope in 1970 must go down in political history as the funniest. Accompanying Nixon on the trip was US Secretary of Defence, Melvin Laird. At the time of the visit, America was at war with Vietnam, and, since Laird had been the brains behind the carpet-bombing of North Vietnam, it was thought judicious that he stay at the hotel, while Nixon and his entourage drove to the Vatican. Laird, however, had other ideas.

Arriving at the papal chamber, the presidential party was surprised to see that Laird was already there, standing around outside and smoking a huge cigar. He was told that he could stay, but that when the Pope arrived, the cigar would have to be extinguished. Laird duly put the cigar in his pocket as soon as the Pope entered the chamber. Unfortunately for Laird, the cigar was still very much alight. Laird's jacket suddenly went up in flames, and clouds of smoke billowed around his person! Thinking that he would save the day by frantically slapping his pocket and extinguishing the fire, all those around Laird mistook what was happening for enthusiastic applause

and began clapping too. In the words of Henry Kissinger: 'Only wisdom accumulated over two millenniums enabled the Vatican officials to pretend that nothing unusual was going on.'

PILLS FOR THE MEMORY

A lady in her mid-forties, following the advice of a friend, invested in some ginkgo biloba, said to counteract the effects of ageing and to aid both short- and long-term memory. The parcel arrived and the woman dutifully took a couple of pills, before placing the rest of the boxes in her bathroom cabinet. For weeks afterwards, she would go up to her bathroom and stare at the packages, not remembering for the life of her why she had bought them in the first place.

BEAUTY AND THE BEAST

An extremely wealthy seventy-year-old widower called Nigel shows up at his Country Club with a breathtakingly beautiful and very sexy twenty-five-year-old woman, who hangs on to his arm and listens intently to his every word.

His friends at the club are all envious. They corner him and ask, 'Nigel, where on earth did you get the trophy girlfriend?'

Nigel replies, 'Girlfriend? She's my wife!'

The old men are bowled over, but continue to quiz him. 'So, how did you persuade her to marry you?'

Nigel says, 'I lied about my age.'

The other members cry, 'What do you mean? Did you tell her you were only fifty?'

Nigel smiles and says, 'No, I told her I was ninety.'

SOS

According to the poet and critic G. K. Chesterton, he was just as prone to a senior moment or two as the rest of us.

Having boarded a train on his way to make a speech, Chesterton was forced to alight in order to send a telegram home to his wife stating, 'Am in Market Harborough. Where ought I to be?'

NO WAY

The eminent conductor Sir Malcolm Sargent was a terrible stickler for manners. One day, whilst visiting the BBC's sound studios in Maida Vale, he announced that a famous friend of his was going to visit and that this friend must be allowed a seat in the control room. The famous guest duly arrived and was warmly welcomed by the studio manager, who ushered him into a seat. During a break in rehearsals, Sargent entered the room to greet his visitor. Turning to the studio manager, Sargent said, 'I would like to introduce you to my friend, the King of Sweden.'

A deathly hush followed, broken only by the distinguished gentleman himself, who said, 'Norway, actually.'

EXISTENTIAL ANGST

'I feel nothing except a certain difficulty in
continuing to exist.'

– BERNARD DE FONTENELLE, MATHEMATICIAN

HOW TAXING

No one likes paying bills and, in particular, no one likes paying the
taxman, but in 1994, several companies in Washington D. C. were
astonished to find their tax payments returned, with a notification
on the envelope stating 'Box Closed for Non-Payment of Rent'.
Apparently the tax office had forgotten to pay the annual fee to
keep the PO Box open.

SLAP HAPPY

One day, Marie Righton was telling her daughter about a
date she'd recently been on with an eighty-nine-year-old
gentleman called Harry.

'The date was okay, but believe it or not I had to slap him
three times during the course of the meal!'

'That's awful,' replied Marie's daughter. 'How come? Was
he being very rude?'

'Oh no,' explained Marie. 'I had to slap his face to keep
him awake!'

ON THE COUCH

A forgetful man goes to see a psychiatrist.

'My trouble is,' he says, 'that I keep forgetting things.'

'How long has this been going on?' asks the psychiatrist.

'How long has what been going on?' replies the man.

HOW CATTY

Two elderly gentlemen, Robin and Bert, were driving through countryside one day when Robin spotted a sign which said: 'CAUTION. SLOW CATS.'

'Poor creatures,' said Bert. 'Do you think one of them has broken its leg?'

ALWAYS LOOK ON THE BRIGHT SIDE

An old man goes to the doctor's and the doctor says, 'I've got bad news and I've got worse news. The bad news is you've got Alzheimer's. The worse news is you've got an inoperable heart condition and you'll be dead in two months.'

And the old man says, 'Well, at least I don't have Alzheimer's.'

GOOD INNINGS

Three old men were discussing what their grandchildren would be saying about them in fifty years.

'I would like my grandchildren to say that I was successful in business,' declared the first man.

'Fifty years from now,' said the second, 'I want my grandchildren to say that I was a devoted family man.'

Turning to the third gentleman, the first man asked, 'So what do you want them to say about you in fifty years?'

'Me?' asked the third man, pondering for a while. 'I want them to say that I look good for my age!'

WATER MISUNDERSTANDING

An elderly gentleman was having a few physical problems and decided to pay a visit to his doctor. The doctor told the old man that he had to drink lukewarm water one hour before breakfast every day.

At the end of a week, the man returned for another doctor's appointment. The concerned doctor asked the old man kindly if he was feeling better. The man answered that he actually felt worse.

The doctor asked, 'Did you drink warm water an hour before breakfast each day?'

'No,' replied the man, grimacing. 'All I could manage was fifteen minutes.'

THE PORTRAIT OF A LADY

An elderly woman decided to have her portrait commissioned. Before the artist had set up his easel, the old woman imparted a few instructions; she wanted to be painted with diamond-encrusted earrings, a diamond necklace, sapphire bracelets, an emerald brooch and a gold watch.

'But you're not wearing any of those things!' the artist exclaimed.

'I know,' the woman said. 'It's just in case I should die before my husband. I'm sure he will find another wife soon, and I want to send his new wife round the bend looking for all that jewellery.'

GOD

A grandfather was sitting with his young granddaughter when the young girl asked, 'Did God make you, Grandpa?'

'Yes, God made me,' the old man replied.

'Did God make me too?'

'Yes, He did,' the old man answered.

For a few minutes, the little girl studied her grandfather, as well as her own reflection in the mirror, while her grandfather wondered what she was thinking about.

At last, the little girl piped up, 'You know, Grandpa,' she said, 'God's doing a much better job recently.'

CANNED LAUGHTER

An old woman was arrested for shoplifting at a supermarket. When she appeared before the judge, the judge asked what she had taken. The lady replied, 'A can of pineapple chunks.'

The judge then asked why she had done it. She replied, 'I was hungry and forgot to bring any money out with me.' The judge asked how many pineapple chunks there were in the tin.

The woman thought for a moment and replied that there were seven chunks in the tin.

The judge said, 'Well then, I'm going to give you seven days in jail – one day for each pineapple.'

As the judge was about to drop his gavel, the lady's husband raised his hand and asked if he might speak. The judge said, 'Yes, what do you have to add?' The husband said, 'She also stole a can of peas.'

UP CLOSE AND PERSONAL

Two elderly men met up for a drink in their local pub. After chatting for a while, they began to discuss a mutual acquaintance.

'Have you seen Paul lately?'

'Well, I have and I haven't.'

'What do you mean by that?'

'Well, I saw a fellow who I thought was Paul and he saw a fellow that he thought was me. And when we got up close to one another . . . it was neither of us.'

FIRED UP

There are many stories surrounding newspaper magnate Robert Maxwell, but none illustrates the senior moment more perfectly than the following.

Maxwell hated anyone smoking in any of his numerous companies, so when he got into a lift one day and discovered a man smoking a cigarette, he was incensed. Immediately, he asked the man how much he earned a week.

'Seventy-five pounds,' the man replied.

Consequently, Maxwell pulled out his wallet and produced three hundred pounds, which he handed over to the man in lieu of a month's wages.

'You're fired,' he said. 'Now get out of my sight!'

All very well and good, but little did Maxwell know that the man was not one of his employees, but instead, he was simply a visitor to the building . . .

CLEAN BILL OF HEALTH

On visiting her friend, Judy, in hospital last August, an elderly woman called Daisy was sitting by the bedside when a woman pushing a huge machine entered the ward. The machine looked extremely frightening with lots of switches attached and tubes coming out of it.

'My God!' exclaimed Daisy. 'That looks horrific. I hope you're not going to plug Judy into that, are you?'

'I hope not as well,' replied the young woman. 'Because this machine is for polishing floors!'

STANDING TO ATTENTION

A very elderly and frail gentleman turned to his equally old friend, Ernest, and asked if he could remember the name of the stuff the army used to put in their cups of tea during World War One, to stop the soldiers getting randy in the trenches. His companion remembered the ingredient, but was unable to recall its name. He asked, however, why his friend wanted to know. The answer was, 'Well, you know, Ernie, I think it's finally started to work.'

A LOT OF BALLS

The most famous cricketing senior moment in broadcasting history must surely be Brian Johnston's insightful words during the Oval Test against the West Indies in 1976, when Michael Holding was bowling to Peter Willey. Observed Johnston of the action on pitch: 'The bowler's Holding, the batsman's Willey.'

Another cricketing senior moment was experienced by the writer and journalist Christopher Martin-Jenkins, who, during the 1979 Cricket World Cup, was heard to say of the appalling weather conditions: 'It is extremely cold here. The England fielders are keeping their hands in their pockets between balls.'

MULTITASKING

'Right now I'm having amnesia and déjà vu at the same time.
I think I've forgotten this before.'
— STEVEN WRIGHT, COMEDIAN

SMOOTH EXIT

Everyone experiences bad days – days when nothing goes right,
days when we drop things on the floor, break our glasses and lose
the car keys. However, imagine the following event, which
happened to a woman called Claire McCormick.

While working at a prominent law firm in the City of London one
day, Claire was summoned by her boss to a meeting in which she
was to be introduced to some important new clients the company
had just taken on. Walking into the room, Claire's boss introduced
her to everyone as one of his best and most efficient
senior executives.

'Claire is a very conscientious,
hard-working member of staff,' he
said. 'What she doesn't know
about our firm isn't worth
knowing. I can't praise this
woman highly enough. She
graduated from Oxford with a first-
class honours degree in law. She
has also studied at the

London School of Economics and has just won three highly controversial libel trials for us.'

'Very pleased to meet you,' chorused the entire room.

Claire was a little flustered at all the flattery, but nonetheless she managed to shake everyone's hands and say that she was looking forward to working for them before exiting the room. The only trouble was that, in her hurry to leave, she had opened the door to a cupboard instead of to the outside offices and walked straight inside. Exiting the meeting with her dignity intact proved difficult.

HONK FOR JESUS

A little old lady from Texas, USA, wrote the following letter to her son:

Dear Aaron,

The other day I went to a local Christian bookstore and saw in the window a 'Honk if you love Jesus' bumper sticker.

I had just come from a thrilling choir practice, followed by a fantastic prayer meeting, so I bought the sticker and put it on my bumper. And I am so glad that I did, for the afternoon that followed was truly a spiritual experience and I felt that the Good Lord Himself was looking down on me.

I was stopped at a red light at a busy intersection, lost in thought about the Lord and how good He is and so I didn't notice that the light had changed. It is a good thing some other kind Christian soul loves Jesus too because if he hadn't honked, I'd never have noticed!

In fact, as I continued driving, I discovered that hundreds of people out there love Jesus! Why, while I was sitting there, the guy behind started honking like crazy, and then he leaned out of his window and screamed. 'For the love of God! Go! Go! Jesus Christ, go!'

Just as this man showed his love for God, everyone else started honking too! I leaned out of my window and started waving and smiling at all these loving people. I even honked my horn a few times to share in the love!'

A GRAVE MISTAKE

In 2006, when the leader of the opposition in Australia, the Hon. Kim Beazley MP, tried to express his condolences to Rove McManus on the day of his wife's funeral, he made the following statement: 'Today our thoughts and the thoughts of many, many Australians will be with Karl Rove as he goes through the  very sad process of burying his wife.' The day of his wife's funeral was not really the best moment to confuse McManus with the American Republican strategist Karl Rove.

ETERNAL YOUTH

'I will never be an old man. To me, old age is always fifteen years older than I am.'
– BERNARD BARUCH, FINANCIER

DECLINING FACULTIES

Mark Twain succinctly summed up the perils of senior moments when he observed that: 'When I was younger, I could remember anything, whether it had happened or not; but my faculties are decaying now and soon I shall be so I cannot remember any but the things that never happened.'

GARDENER'S WORLD

Phoebe Walker swore that her garden was the only thing that kept her from going insane. She had four children, two dogs, three cats and several rabbits, ducks and guinea pigs to look after, not to mention a husband who doted on her. She also worked part-time as a bookkeeper and served as a member of several local-interest groups, as well as fulfilling her many commitments as secretary to the local parish council. Despite having all this to occupy her, Phoebe's garden remained her prize and joy; she was particularly proud of her vegetable patch, in which she grew prize-winning

marrows and runner beans, and her orchard with its huge variety of apple and plum trees.

On one particular occasion, having put on her wellies and picked up various implements from her shed, Phoebe trudged down to the bottom of her garden to get on with a job that she had been postponing for some time. The problem was that when she got there, she couldn't remember what this job was. Standing there, deep in thought for some time, Phoebe's mind was a complete blank, so she decided to go back to the house and make herself a cup of tea. This helped to achieve the desired result, as Phoebe suddenly remembered what it was she had to do and, mug in hand, she rushed down to the bottom of the garden, only to find once again that she had forgotten the purpose of her trip. Infuriated with herself, Phoebe now decided that instead of returning to the house, she would sit on a bench she had recently purchased, enjoy the rest of her cup of tea and no doubt she would recall what it was she had come to do.

Two hours later, Phoebe awoke with a start. The sun had gone in and she had upset her mug of tea, so that there was a huge stain in the middle of her dress. Feeling something wet and sloppy on her forehead, she tentatively put her hand to it, only to discover that a bird had pooed on her during her slumbers. Making her way back to the house in disgust as it began to rain, a bedraggled Phoebe entered the kitchen to hear someone knocking at the front door.

In one great thunderbolt of recognition, as if the heavens had miraculously opened up, Phoebe suddenly recalled what it was she had been meaning to do at the bottom of the garden. Running to the door, Phoebe flung it open, only to be met by the vicar, who had stopped by to collect a basket of fruit and vegetables for the next day's Harvest Festival celebrations.

TWICE AS FORGETFUL

An elderly couple were going away on holiday and stopped at a roadside restaurant for lunch. After the meal, the elderly woman left her glasses on the table, but she didn't notice they were missing until they were back on the road. By this time, the old couple had to travel quite a distance before they could find a place to turn around.

The elderly man complained all the way back to the restaurant and muttered under his breath, calling his wife every terrible name he could think of. When the pair finally arrived at the restaurant, and the old woman got out of the car to retrieve her glasses, her husband shouted after her, 'And while you're in there, you might as well get my teeth, too.'

PUBLISHING PITFALLS

For several years, Francis McClure had worked in a publishing house as an editor. Francis had always prided himself on his skills as a wordsmith. He could, or so he boasted, spot a typo at five hundred paces and his proofreading skills were apparently second to none.

For these reasons, Francis was the obvious choice to edit a book by a very famous author, and was charged not only with overseeing the inside text, but also with writing the book's cover copy. Weeks passed by and Francis slaved away over the proofs, raising his head every now and then to tell his colleagues just how interesting it was and what a marvellous job he was doing on the text. Every now and then someone would offer to help, but Francis was adamant that no one else was to touch 'his' book and, consequently, everyone kept clear.

Finally, the book was sent off to the printers and several weeks later advanced copies arrived at the office. The box was unpacked and Francis proudly held up the first copy for everyone to admire.

Silence.

'What's wrong with you all? It looks brilliant,' Francis exclaimed.

'Yes,' came the swift reply, 'except for one minor detail. You've forgotten to put the author's name on the jacket.'

BEDROOM BRAWL

Senior moments can quite often be physically painful. After all, if you're not wearing your spectacles, you stand the risk of not only tripping over objects, but also walking into lampposts or down potholes. One sixty-six-year-old man from Toronto in Canada went to his doctor in order to consult him about a pain he was experiencing in his left calf muscle. The doctor examined him thoroughly and gave him an X-ray. In fact, he did everything he could to find out the cause of the pain, but could not come up with an answer. Eventually, he sent the man away with some painkillers and told him to come back in a week's time if the pain hadn't subsided.

A few nights later, the man was woken up in the middle of the night suffering acute pain in his left leg, having just been kicked violently by his wife.

'Ouch! Don't do that,' he said. 'That's just where my leg hurts.'

'But that's where I always kick you when you're snoring,' she cried.

TROUBLE AND STRIFE

An elderly gentleman pays a visit to a wizard to ask him to remove a curse he has been living with for the last forty years. The wizard tells the man that he needs to know the exact words that were used when the curse was put on him in the first place. The old man replies without a moment's hesitation, 'I now pronounce you man and wife.'

NO LAUGHING MATTER

The nineteenth-century dentist Horace Wells once attended a scientific conference at which he saw laughing gas being demonstrated. Immediately realizing the gas's potential, Wells decided to use it on his own patients. Within a month he had tested it out on fifteen people. However, when Wells decided to give a demonstration at the Massachusetts General Hospital by removing a patient's tooth while putting them under the influence of the gas, he hadn't reckoned on the fact that senior momentitus can strike at any time. Forgetting to give the unfortunate patient enough nitrous oxide to kill the pain, Wells was horrified when the boy began roaring his head off and crying. To add insult to injury, Wells's blunder also cost him the respect of his peers, who labelled the experiment a 'humbug affair'.

LADY DIANA COOPER

Invited to a musical gala to celebrate the hundredth birthday of musical benefactor Sir Robert Mayer, Lady Diana Cooper is said to have grown a little confused when she came across a rather lovely woman who seemed familiar to her, but to whom she couldn't put a name. The two women enjoyed a brief conversation when suddenly it dawned upon Lady Diana that she was talking to the Queen. 'I sank into a curtsey and said, "I'm terribly sorry, Ma'am, but I didn't recognize you without your crown on."'

GARDEN OF DELIGHTS

An elderly gentleman by the name of Alfred had recently retired and had decided to spend his dotage living on a large farm in the country. One evening, he decided to visit the lake around the back of the house as it was a tranquil and secluded spot, the perfect place to while away a midsummer evening. Drone flies droopily swung across the surface and all around the trees were filled with sweet summer foliage. On this particular evening, however, Alfred was surprised to hear feminine voices shouting and laughing with delight, along with the frequent splashing of water. As he got nearer to the pond, he saw that there was a group of young women skinny-dipping there.

Alfred at once made the women aware of his presence and they all swam hurriedly to the far side of the pond. One of the braver women shouted to him, 'We're not coming out until you leave.'

The old man replied, 'I didn't come here to watch you ladies swim or to make you get out of the pond naked. I only came down here to feed the alligator.'

SICK HUMOUR

Mrs Green called her doctor's surgery to find out her husband's test results.

'I'm so sorry,' the nurse told her, 'but there's been some sort of mistake. When we sent your husband's samples to the laboratory, some samples from another Mr Green were sent as well. One Mr Green has tested positive for Alzheimer's disease and the other Mr Green for syphilis. We can't tell which results are your husband's.'

'That's terrible,' cried Mrs Green. 'Can we do the test over again to find the answer?'

'Your Health Maintenance Organization won't pay for these expensive tests to be run twice.'

'Well, what are we supposed to do?'

'The doctor recommends that you drop your husband off in the middle of town. If he finds his way home, don't sleep with him.'

MUSIC THERAPY

'You face certain things as you get older and think, "Well, time is running out." I do like to keep the brain working. I learn poetry for that. And playing the piano is a good mental and physical exercise in co-ordination.'
— ANTHONY HOPKINS, ACTOR

MUSICAL MISHAPS

A minister in the Church of England was paying a visit to one of his elderly parishioners one day. She showed him into her front parlour and while she was in the kitchen making a pot of tea, the minister noticed a glass bowl filled with water with something floating on top, sitting on the piano. Going up to the bowl, the minister realized that the floating object was a condom! Taken aback, he waited for the woman to come back into the room and then asked politely what it was she had placed on top of her piano.

'Oh that!' replied the woman. 'I was walking back from the shops recently when I saw it lying on the pavement. There were instructions printed on it saying, "Place on organ to prevent infectious diseases." I don't have an organ, but I thought the piano would do just as well, and do you know, I haven't been ill all winter!'

SENIOR SEX

While acquainting herself with a new elderly patient, a young nurse enquired of the old lady: 'How long have you been bedridden?'

'Why, not for about twenty years . . . when my husband was alive,' she replied.

YOU MUST BE KIDDING

One day, the famous author and literary critic Edmund Gosse was travelling on a bus when he saw a lady getting on, whom he recognized as the headmistress of a local school. The woman sat down next to a respectable-looking gentleman, whom Gosse knew was a local solicitor. The lady turned to him and announced loudly, 'I can see you don't know who I am, but you are the father of one of my children!'

'TO DO' LIST

'There was a time in my life, decades ago, when I was so full of energy that I was not only going to end world hunger, but also stop war and eliminate racism. Whereas today my life goals, to judge from the notes I leave myself, tend to be along the lines of "buy detergent".'

– DAVE BARRY, COMEDIAN

IRREVERENT HUMOUR

The priest's sermon was on the Ten Commandments. When the priest had reached the fourth, 'Thou shalt not steal', he noticed that one of his parishioners, a little old man sitting in the front row, suddenly became very agitated. When the preacher reached the seventh commandment, 'Thou shalt not commit adultery', the man suddenly smiled and relaxed.

When the mass had ended, the priest approached the man and asked him the reason for his strange behaviour. The man replied with an embarrassed smile, 'When you talked about the fourth commandment, "Thou shalt not steal", I suddenly discovered that my wallet was missing. But when you said, "Thou shalt not commit adultery", I suddenly remembered where I'd left it.'

MODEL BEHAVIOUR

At London Fashion Week, actor and television personality Stephen Fry insisted that he overheard one of the function's organizers apologizing for the appalling backstage conditions. Apparently, she was particularly concerned to point out that although they had a lavatory, it had no door.

'But how,' wailed one fashionista, 'am I supposed to get in then?'

A THESPIAN NEVER FORGETS

'I have a memory like an elephant.
In fact, elephants
often consult me.'

– NOEL COWARD, ACTOR AND PLAYWRIGHT

LITERARY LOSSES

In 1919, T. E. Lawrence (otherwise known as Lawrence of Arabia) lost most of *The Seven Pillars of Wisdom* while changing trains at Reading, England. Having left the pages on the first train, he was unfortunately already on the second train by the time he realized his mistake, and it was too late to recover them. Instead, Lawrence had to rewrite the book from memory.

Similarly, Ernest Hemingway's wife, Hadley, had an almost identical experience whilst travelling through France. The author of *A Farewell to Arms* and *The Old Man and the Sea* had entrusted his wife with a suitcase containing all of his early manuscripts, excluding three short stories. Hadley, however, lost the suitcase whilst on the train, thus causing one of literature's most tragic losses due to senior momentitus.

The nineteenth-century poet Algernon Charles Swinburne also suffered a nasty 'transport versus manuscript' moment when, in 1868, he left his invaluable manuscript of the tragedy *Bothwell* in a hansom cab. However, realizing his mistake, Swinburne advertised the loss and offered a reward for its safe return. Shortly afterwards, manuscript and author were happily reunited.

HOME SWEET HOME

Irwin Edman, a lecturer in philosophy at Columbia University, is said to have once visited the home of one of his colleagues for an evening meal. By two o'clock in the morning, the colleague, who was feeling more than a little tired, began to yawn in the hope that Edman would get the hint and go home. Sadly, however, the philosopher did not understand what his host was getting at and eventually the man said, 'Irwin, I hate asking you to leave, but I'm giving a lecture first thing tomorrow morning. I have to get up very early.' To which the philosopher is said to have replied, 'Oh my God! I'm so sorry. I thought you were in my house!'

MORNING MADNESS

Writing to a friend, the author G. K. Chesterton described his morning routine thus: 'On rising this morning, I carefully washed my boots in hot water and blackened my face, poured coffee on my sardines, and put my hat on the fire to boil. These activities will give you some idea of my state of mind . . . '

THE PRIME OF LIFE
'I am in the prime of senility.'
— BENJAMIN FRANKLIN, WRITER AND POLITICIAN

SMOKING HAZARDS

A young man by the name of Pierre was feeling suicidal. His girlfriend of six years had just dumped him, he'd failed to get a promotion at work and his landlord had told him he wasn't going to renew the lease on his flat. Feeling extremely low, Pierre sat down in his kitchen, where, having written out letters to his friends and family explaining his decision, he had decided to put an end to his suffering by switching on the gas oven. This he did and afterwards sat back down to await his fate. Only then did he decide that he wanted one last cigarette for old time's sake. Feeling in his coat pocket for the packet, he withdrew one and proceeded to light it. BOOM! A mighty explosion tore through the room. Pierre had forgotten about all the leaked gas. The explosion destroyed not only his kitchen and apartment, but also several neighbours' apartments, though luckily no one was hurt and Pierre survived.

WHERE THERE'S A WILL

An elderly gentleman had serious hearing problems for years. He went to the doctor and was fitted with a number of hearing aids, which allowed him to regain full hearing. The old man returned to his doctor one month later and the doctor said, 'Your hearing is perfect. Your family must be really pleased that you can hear again.' The old man smiled and replied, 'Oh, I haven't told them yet. I just sit around and listen to their conversations. I've changed my will four times.'

OFF HER TROLLEY

When out shopping at her local supermarket, an elderly woman forgot where she'd parked. A nearby police officer, noticing her agitation, asked, 'Is something wrong?'

'I can't find my car,' she explained.

'What kind is it?' he enquired sympathetically.

The old lady gave him a quizzical look. 'Name some.'

IMMORTAL SIN

In 1632, Barker and Lucas were the king's own printers, but when they typeset the Bible and printed 1,000 copies, they were horrified to discover that they had omitted the rather crucial word 'not' in the seventh commandment so that it read, 'thou shalt commit adultery'. Subsequently, the two men were prosecuted and fined £3,000 for their mistake.

AMOROUS RECALL

The actress Ethel Barrymore was once told that an actress acquaintance had, prior to getting married, made a full confession to her prospective husband regarding her past love affairs. 'What honesty! What courage,' somebody apparently remarked, but the only comment Barrymore made was, 'What a memory!'

THE TRIALS OF OLD AGE

'He [Dr Johnson] observed, "There is a wicked inclination in most people to suppose an old man decayed in his intellects. If a young or middle-aged man, when leaving a company, does not recollect where he laid his hat, it is nothing; but if the same inattention is discovered in an old man, people will shrug their shoulders, and say, 'His memory is going.'"'
– JAMES BOSWELL, *LIFE OF JOHNSON*

WEEK DAZE

Prime Minister Benjamin Disraeli once called on an acquaintance, Lady Bradford, and was informed that she had gone into town, as she normally did every Monday morning.

'I thought that you would know, sir,' the servant is reported to have said.

'I did not,' replied Disraeli, 'nor did I know that it was Monday.'

OLD MAN

An old man visited his doctor in order to get some test results from the previous week. 'I've got some good news and some bad news,' said the doctor.

'Give me the good news first!' replied the patient.

'The good news is that you have only twenty-four hours to live.'

'Oh my God!' cried the patient. 'If that's the good news, then what's the bad news?'

'I forgot to call you yesterday,' said the doctor.

INVISIBILITY

There are some compensations to growing older and realizing you have more senior moments than good nights out. For example, people don't notice you as much, which can, as Germaine Greer so aptly points out, be desirable: 'There are tremendous upsides to being invisible. You can observe, you can watch. Life is more interesting. When you're self-involved and you see yourself centre stage all the time, you're in agonies of self-consciousness, you're really concerned: "How do I look? How do I sound?" It's wonderful not to care about that any more.'

HOTBED OF CONFUSION

One day, a travel agent called Samuel saw an elderly couple peering into his shop window, looking at all the posters of beautiful beaches and luxury five-star hotels. Samuel had sold a lot of holidays that week and was feeling quite generous, and, as the old couple looked so downcast and grey, he knew it was his duty to help.

Ushering the old couple into the shop, the travel agent asked them to sit down and said, 'This is your lucky day. I know that on your pensions you couldn't possibly afford a holiday, but I'd like you to accept my gift to you at a wonderful resort in Italy, no expense spared, all paid for by me.' The old couple were extremely surprised, even more so when Samuel asked his secretary to book the flights and the five-star hotel room.

One month later, the little old lady came back to Samuel's shop alone.

'And how did you enjoy the holiday, madam?' Samuel asked excitedly.

'Oh, I had a marvellous time. The hotel was splendid. The room was beautiful with fantastic views over the sea, but there was something puzzling me. Who was that old man I had to share a bed with?'

SIGN LANGUAGE

Signs are there to make things simpler, to make things easier, to make things clearer – or are they? Well, not if you're the person responsible for the sign inside one university's halls of residence, which reads: 'Remember always to close the window and lock the door before leaving the room.' Whoever wrote this was obviously suffering a senior moment – or perhaps it was a lecturer hoping never to see any of their students again?

RIPE OLD AGE

Although this collection of senior moments is packed full of anecdotes highlighting the less kindly side of growing old, there are plenty of examples of sprightly OAPs. Take, for example, the following description of Princess Alice, the last surviving granddaughter of Queen Victoria, who at the time the description was written in 1976 was ninety-six years old:

Princess Alice still makes an occasional official appearance, although she is a bit frail. But not too frail to read without eyeglasses, not too frail to make an occasional shopping sortie by bus, not too frail to attend Sunday services at St Mary Abbots Church near her house in Kensington. When friends pressed her to carry a walking stick, she reluctantly agreed, but she had it disguised as an umbrella.

– R. W. APPLE, JOURNALIST

DOH!

One burglar had to have been suffering from a terrible senior moment when, after having robbed a petrol station, he left his mobile phone behind, allowing police to trace their man within hours of the crime.

POTATO HEAD

In the 1990s, US Vice President Dan Quayle was second only to America's present-day president George W. Bush when it came to making foolish errors. Visiting a school in 1992, the politician walked into a classroom and, in front of not only the whole class, but also the press, proceeded to walk up to the blackboard and correct a little boy's spelling of 'potato' to 'potatoe'.

PARTING SHOT

'When I was forty, my doctor advised me that a man in his forties shouldn't play tennis. I heeded his advice carefully and could hardly wait until I reached fifty to start again.'
– HUGO LAFAYETTE BLACK, POLITICIAN

MEMORY LAPSE

Two old men are chatting. One man says, 'My friend, you must try this memory pill I'm taking. I remember absolutely everything, it's amazing.'

The other man says, 'It sounds wonderful. What's the name of the pill?'

The first man replies, 'The name of the pill? Well, let's see. What's the name of that small white flower with a yellow centre? It begins with "D" . . .'

The other man says, 'A daisy?'

The first man says, 'Yes, that's right!' Then, calling for his wife, he says, 'Daisy, what is the name of that pill I'm taking?'

SENIOR SPORT

Keeping active is a prerequisite if you want to enjoy a ripe old age and keep everyone else on their toes. Follow the example of Adolph Zukor, Chairman Emeritus of Paramount Film Studios, who was ninety-eight when he made the following observation: 'The doctors don't want me to be active. Ha! Why, in New York, two or three times a week, weather permitting, I jump into a cab and go to my office . . . Infirmity is a state of mind. I sleep well because I don't let my mind get stale.'

SLOW COACH

An old gentleman was driving on the motorway at his usual speed, which was far too slow. A police officer pulled him over and said, 'I guess you know why I stopped you, sir?'

'Sure I do,' the old gentleman replied, 'I was the only one you could catch!'

LOST IN THE POST

In December 2006, newspapers reported a story concerning a letter received by the Post Office that had been sent to an address in Bude in the south-west of England. The letter had the name of the recipient printed on the front, but underneath, where the address should have been, there was nothing but an arrow pointing to a drawing of the West Country with the message 'somewhere here' printed underneath. Miraculously, the Post Office managed to deliver the letter to its rightful recipient, however the sender – an old work colleague of his who wanted to get back in touch – had forgotten to put a return address on his letter!

DEAD SORRY

A clergyman once complained to George Eliot, author of *Middlemarch*, *Adam Bede* and *Daniel Deronda*, that while reading her *Scenes of a Clerical Life*, he had recognized himself in one of the less pleasant characters.

'I'm so sorry,' the author is said to have replied. 'I thought you were dead.'

ROYAL FLUSH

The great conductor Sir Thomas Beecham is reported to have once returned to his hotel in Manchester, only to come across a woman in the lobby. Beecham knew that he had seen her before, but unfortunately could not recall what her name was or where it had been that they'd met. In fact, the only thing he could recall about her was that the woman had a brother and so, bearing this in mind, he asked how her brother was and whether he was still in the same job. The woman smiled and said, 'Oh yes. He is very well – and still the king.'

ANOTHER CASE OF MISTAKEN IDENTITY

One day, the actor Douglas Fairbanks was driving back to his home in Beverly Hills, Los Angeles, when he came across a respectable-looking gentleman, whose face he recognized but whose name he couldn't remember, walking alongside the road. Stopping the car, Fairbanks asked the man if he could give him a lift. The man, looking somewhat surprised, but exceedingly grateful, accepted the offer in a rather posh English accent. Still Fairbanks couldn't remember the man's name. Nevertheless, they chatted all the way back to Fairbanks's mansion, where the film star asked the man if he'd like to join him inside for a drink. The man again accepted the offer and the two chatted away as before, with Fairbanks all the time trying to recall his guest's name. Infuriatingly, the guest seemed to know a lot about Fairbanks and about all Fairbanks's friends, but Fairbanks could not place him in any context or situation that would give him a hint as to the man's identity.

Finally, he managed to whisper to his secretary, 'What's this man's name? I think he's Lord someone or other?'

'No, sir, that is your butler. You sacked him last month for being drunk and disorderly.'

THE AGE GAME

A young boy called Joseph asked his grandmother how old she was and she replied, 'Thirty-nine and holding.' Joseph thought for a moment and then said, 'How old would you be if you let go?'

GREAT EGGSPECTATIONS

An elderly married couple went to breakfast at a restaurant in which the 'Senior Special' was two eggs, bacon, sausages and toast for the bargain price of £2.99.

'It sounds great,' said the old woman enthusiastically, 'but I don't want the eggs.'

'Then I'll have to charge you £4.99 because you are ordering à la carte,' the waitress warned her.

'You mean I'd have to pay for not taking the eggs?' the elderly woman asked incredulously. 'In that case, I'll take the special.'

'How would you like your eggs?'

'Raw and in the shell,' the woman replied.

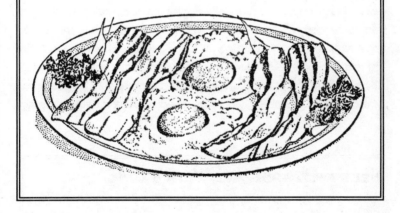

SAY WHAT?

An elderly gentleman was showing off his new hearing aid to a friend.

'This is the finest hearing aid on the market today,' bragged the old fellow. 'I paid £500 for it.'

'What kind is it?' asked his friend.

'Half past five,' came the response.

VIDEO NASTY

When police were called to a robbery at a video store in Toledo, Ohio, they were astonished to find that the thief, far from getting away with the goodies, had instead got himself stuck in an air vent. Not that they could see him at first, but they had observed footprints in the snow leading up to the shop, but none going away, so it was only a matter of elimination to realize their man was still on the premises. The fire brigade was called, and it took them one hour to cut the man free, after which he was arrested and charged.

NEITHER A BORROWER NOR A LENDER BE

Whether the following is a senior moment or simply a case of sheer stupidity is hard to tell, but, according to history, the writer Thomas Carlyle once lent the first volume of his manuscript *The History of the French Revolution* to his friend and fellow author,

John Stuart Mill, who subsequently lent it to his lover so that she could read it too. Unfortunately for everyone concerned, the lover's maid, not being of a literary bent, thought the pages were rubbish and consequently burnt the lot! Agonizing over this mishap, Carlyle wrote a letter to his brother, saying that he felt like a man who had 'nearly killed himself accomplishing nothing'. Nevertheless, with the help of some money given to him by Mill, Carlyle rewrote the entire book, which then went on to guarantee him huge success.

AUTHOR, AUTHOR

The Scottish eighteenth-century author John Campbell wandered into a bookshop one day and became so engrossed in a book that eventually he decided to buy it. Having taken the book home, he read half of it before realizing that the author was none other than himself.

TWO LADIES

Two old ladies were coming out of the Drury Lane Theatre one summer evening, having just been to see Rex Harrison in the stage musical *My Fair Lady*, when one of the women was overheard saying, 'Of course, you know Rex Harrison isn't his real name.' The other lady turned to her friend and was then heard to reply, 'Rex Harrison isn't whose real name, dear?'

COLD FAN

Although popular with his fans, Rex Harrison could cut them very short. Two female fans once stopped him as he was coming out of Drury Lane and asked him for his autograph. He dismissed them with a wave of his hand and called a cab. The fans took exception to this and one of them smacked him around the head with her handbag. This was where his rapport with his fellow actors was shown to be not as friendly as believed. His co-star in *My Fair Lady*, Stanley Holloway, turned to a colleague and said, "That really was the finest case of the fan hitting the shit as you are likely to see!'

STICKY SITUATION

In January 2005, one seventy-eight-year-old grandmother had a lucky escape when she accidentally glued her eyes together. The old woman was defrosting her fridge when she felt her eyes starting to water, so she reached for a bottle of eye drops, but instead of the medicine she picked up a bottle of glue.

'The second my eyes were glued shut,' said the woman, 'I realized the glue was next to the drops in the fridge.' Luckily, her husband was on hand to help. After the lady's husband had dialled for an ambulance, the woman was taken into hospital where she was later unglued and sent home as good as new.

EAT YOUR VEGETABLES

Recent US tests have shown that although eating vegetables is good for slowing the inevitable process of mental decline that takes place with age, eating fruit makes no substantial difference whatsoever. People aged sixty-five and over who ate three servings of vegetables a day saw their rate of mental decline slow by an astonishing 40 per cent, compared with those who ate less than one portion a day. Food for thought, indeed.

TESTING THE DRIVER

Even at the best of times, written tests can bring out our stupid side, but none more so, or so it seems, than the written part of the driving test. Here are a few examples from the California Department of Transportation's driving test.

Q. What is the difference between a flashing red traffic light and a flashing yellow traffic light?
A. The colour.

Q. When driving through fog, what should you use?
A. Your car.

Q. What changes would occur in your lifestyle if you could no longer drive lawfully?
A. I would drive unlawfully.

Q. Would you yield when a blind pedestrian is crossing the road?
A. What for? He can't see my license plate.

Q. What problems would you face if you were arrested for drunk driving?
A. I'd probably lose my buzz a lot faster.

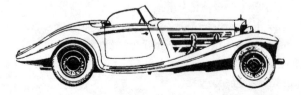

PATCHWORK

During an appointment with his cardiologist, a patient informed his doctor that he was having trouble with one of his medications.

'Which one?' asked the doctor.

'The patch,' replied the patient. 'The nurse told me to put on a new one every six hours and now I'm running out of places to put it!'

The doctor made him quickly undress and discovered that the man had over fifty patches on his body. Now the instructions include removal of the old patch before applying a new one.

AMATEUR PERFORMANCE

American president Ronald Reagan was a dab hand at malapropisms, once referring to Princess Diana as Princess David. In 1943, Warner Brothers released *This Is The Army* starring Ronald Reagan. During shooting, however, Reagan was introduced to the movie's writer a total of five times, but each time the introduction was made, the writer said exactly the same thing: 'You've got a few things to correct – for example, a huskiness of the voice – but you really should give this business some consideration when the war is over.'

Reagan wasn't too impressed. He had already been working in the film industry for six years.

DEAD SERIOUS

An elderly woman was terribly distraught as her husband Ernie had just passed away. Rose went to the undertakers to take one last look at her husband, and as soon as she laid eyes on him, she started crying. The mortician walked over to try to comfort her. Through her tears, Rose explained that she was upset because her husband was wearing a black suit, and it had been his last wish to be buried wearing a blue suit.

The mortician apologized profusely and explained that traditionally they always put bodies in black suits, but as it had been Ernie's special request, he would see what he could do to fix things.

The next day, Rose went along to the morticians to have one final moment alone with Ernie before the funeral, which was taking place the next day.

When at last she saw her husband, she managed a smile as she saw Ernie was sporting a fine blue suit. She said to the mortician, 'That's fantastic, thank you so much . . . but where on earth did you find that beautiful suit?'

'Well,' replied the mortician, pleased to have been of service, 'after you left yesterday, a man about the same size as your husband was brought in and he was wearing a smart blue suit. His wife was crying because she had wanted him buried in a *black* suit.'

Ernie's wife smiled gratefully at the undertaker.

'After that,' he continued, 'it was just a matter of swapping the heads.'

COLD COMFORT

A team of researchers from the Mayo Clinic in Rochester, Minnesota, recently made the fascinating discovery that common viruses may serve to contribute to the phenomenon of senior moments. The research revealed that common viruses picked up every year could be invading the central nervous system and damaging our brains. As the infections accumulate over the years, they allegedly chip away at the brain, resulting years later in memory loss and waning mental ability.

The tests were carried out on mice who had been infected with a virus that resembled polio. It was observed that these mice had difficulty learning how to navigate a maze designed to test their spatial memory skills; and their ability to get around the maze was found to be directly linked to the number of cells the virus had killed in the hippocampus brain region (which plays an important role in memory and learning).

Many people will contract two or three viruses from the picornavirus family every year – these can range from common colds and stomach upsets to more serious complaints such as encephalitis, meningitis and polio.

Study leader Dr Charles Howe said: 'Our study suggests that virus-induced memory loss could accumulate over a lifetime and eventually lead to clinical cognitive memory deficits.'

So next time you suffer a senior moment, take comfort and blame it on your cold.

COLD SWEATS

An elderly married couple went for their annual medical examination together. After the examination, the doctor then said to the elderly man: 'You appear to be in good health. Do you have any medical concerns that you would like to discuss with me?'

'In fact, I do,' replied the man. 'After I have sex with my wife for the first time, I am usually hot and sweaty, but after I have sex with my wife the second time, I am usually cold and shivering.'

'This is very interesting,' replied the doctor. 'Let me do some research and get back to you.'

After examining the old man's wife, the doctor said: 'Everything appears to be fine. Do you have any medical concerns that you would like to discuss with me?' The lady replied that she had no questions nor worries.

The doctor then said: 'Your husband has voiced an unusual concern. He claims that he is usually hot and sweaty after having sex the first time with you and then cold and shivering after the second time. Do you know why?' The old woman laughed wickedly and replied, 'That's because the first time is usually in July and the second time is usually in December!'

MORE LATE BLOOMERS

As the years go by, all of us will suffer a senior moment or two, of that there can be no doubt, but wouldn't it be nice to feel that even though we are growing older and more senile, there is still plenty to do, still a whole range of opportunities to achieve great things? Here are some examples of late achievers to inspire you.

- Carmela Bousada, who gave birth to twin boys seven days before her sixty-seventh birthday, is the oldest woman to become a new mum.

- NASA astronaut John Glenn, aged seventy-seven, is the oldest man to have gone into space.

- Takao Arayama, aged seventy, is reportedly the oldest man to have climbed Mount Everest.

- Lord Palmerston was the oldest man to become British prime minister when he took over the post at the age of seventy-one.

- The oldest man to be elected to the post of US president was Ronald Reagan, who was first elected at the tender age of sixty-eight.

- At age eighty-two, Carol Channing, famous for her Broadway hit *Hello, Dolly!*, proved that you are never too old to fall in love. After she wrote about her first love, Harry Kullijian, in her autobiography, Mr Kullijian read the book and phoned up his childhood sweetheart. Shortly afterwards, the couple became engaged.

- The godfather of trashy fiction, Sydney Sheldon, who wrote novels such as *The Naked Face*, *The Other Side of Midnight* and *Rage of Angels*, did not start his writing career until he was in his fifties, proving that it's never to late too become a success.

PULL OVER

An old woman was speeding down a motorway, greatly exceeding the speed limit. She was knitting at the same time, with her hands between the spokes of the steering wheel. A police car overtook her in the outside lane with all its lights flashing. As it drew level with her, a policeman wound down his window and shouted to her, 'Pull over.'

'No,' she shouted back. 'Pair of socks!'

FURTHER SIGNS YOU ARE GETTING ON . . .

- Everything hurts, and what doesn't hurt, doesn't work.

- The gleam in your eyes is from the sun hitting your bifocals.

- You feel like it's the morning after the night before, and you haven't been anywhere.

- Your children begin to look middle-aged.

- You know all the answers, but nobody asks you the questions.

- Your knees buckle, but your belt won't.

- Dialling a long-distance call wears you out.

- The best part of the day is over when your alarm clock goes off.

- A fortune teller wants to read your face.

- You get your exercise acting as a pall-bearer.

- You have too much room in the house and not enough in the medicine cabinet.

A DAMN GOOD REMEDY

If you're getting on a bit and having one too many senior moments, perhaps you should take a leaf out of Wilbur Smith's book. 'My new wife is thirty-two and I'm seventy. She's rejuvenated me totally. It's so exciting to see life through the eyes of a modern girl.'

THE PERKS OF SENIOR MOMENTITUS

It is reassuring to know that something as troublesome as senior momentitus can have a few perks . . .

- You can throw yourself a surprise party – just invite everyone you know, then forget all about it.

- You can buy your own Christmas presents, wrap them and not have a clue what they are when you come to open them.

- You can bake your own birthday cake and still imagine someone else has done it for you.

BABY, BABY

A fifty-one-year-old woman went to Italy to see a doctor who could help elderly women have babies. She soon fell pregnant and gave birth to a beautiful boy. All her friends and acquaintances loved the child, but one day one of her closest friends had to move away, so she decided to make one last visit to see her friend's child. The woman told her friend that the child was asleep, but that he would wake up soon and then she could cuddle him. However, as the hours passed by, the friend grew increasingly impatient. Finally, the new mother owned up.

'I have to wait for him to wake up and cry because I can't remember where I put him down to sleep!' she confessed sheepishly.

PAST YOUR BEDTIME

Sometimes you are responsible for your own senior moments and sometimes senior moments are simply thrust upon you. One senior citizen wrote to *The Times* to report the following event: 'One Saturday we decided, with two friends, that we would like to go to a midnight movie at the local cinema. I rang to book the seats and mentioned that we were all OAPs. "Madam," was the reply, "there are no reductions at this time of night – you should all be in bed."'

LIFE IMITATING ART

Aberdeen Press and Journal recently reported that a diary reader on the wrong side of sixty received a letter from Aberdeenshire's library and information service telling him that a book he had requested was available for collection at the Westhill branch near Aberdeen.

It was only after he read the letter that the reader recalled he had already had an automated voice message giving him the same information.

'What with getting sorted for Christmas,' said the reader, 'I completely forgot about the phone call.'

So what was the book he had requested?

Yes, it was *The Book of Senior Moments* by Shelley Klein.

UNHOLY ERROR

Printers over the centuries have suffered from what can only be deemed chronic senior moments when printing the Bible. Here are a few of the most sinful offenders . . .

- The Bug Bible, 1535: 'Thou shalt not need to be afrayed for eny bugges [instead of 'terror'] by night' – PSALMS 91:5

- The Unrighteous Bible, 1653: 'Know ye not that the unrighteous shall inherit [for 'shall not inherit'] the Kingdom of God' – I CORINTHIANS 6:9

- The Sin On Bible, 1716: 'Sin on more' [instead of 'Sin no more'] – John 5:14

- The Fool Bible, printed during the reign of Charles I: 'The fool hath said in his heart there is a God' [instead of 'there is no God'] – PSALMS 14

- The Idle Bible, 1809: 'The idole shepherd' [instead of 'the idle shepherd'] – ZECHARIAH 11:17

- The Large Family Bible, 1820: 'Shall I bring to the birth and not cease [instead of 'cause'] to bring forth' – ISAIAH 66:9

SPEECH THERAPY

Joseph Addison, founder of *The Spectator*, was a terrible public speaker. He once embarked on a speech at the House of Commons, beginning: 'Mr Speaker, I conceive – I conceive, sire – I conceive . . .' At this point he was interrupted by another member, who quipped: 'The right honourable Secretary of State has conceived thrice, and brought forth nothing.'

ON THE BALL

When Winston Churchill was a very old man, he paid one of his infrequent visits to the House of Commons, of which he was still a member. An MP, observing him, remarked, 'After all, they say he's potty.' Muttered Churchill, 'They say he can't hear either.'

MAD SCIENTIST

Sir Isaac Newton's forgetfulness was legendary. He would forget appointments, forget to comb his hair and forget to eat. Indeed, so obsessed was Newton with scientific study that he would even sometimes forget where he was. Frequently, he would rise in the morning and sit on the edge of his bed for hours, musing over a problem for so long that he forgot to get dressed.

HURT PRYDE

Edith Cavell was an English nurse shot by the Germans for helping Allied prisoners to escape during the First World War. She was hailed as a martyr and a statue of her was erected outside the National Portrait Gallery in London in 1920. The artist James Pryde watched the unveiling of the statue and considered it a poor likeness. When the statue was revealed, he cried, 'My God, they've shot the wrong person!'

GROWING OLD GRACEFULLY

At George Moore's eightieth birthday party, reporters asked the Anglo-Irish novelist how it was that he continued to enjoy such excellent health. Moore answered, 'It's because I never smoked, or drank, or touched a girl until I was eleven years old.'

SET IN STONE

It is said that the following epitaph appears at the bottom of a tombstone in Tasmania: 'Lord she is thin.' The 'e' is on the back of the stone, the monumental mason not having left himself enough room to carve it on the front.

SLIP OF THE TONGUE

A newsreader on the Rhodesian (now Zimbabwe) Broadcasting Corporation once referred to the enormously wealthy Greek shipping tycoon, Aristotle Onassis, as the 'Greek shitting tycoon'.

BIBLIOGRAPHY

Burningham, John (Ed.)
The Time of Your Life – Getting On With Getting On
(Bloomsbury, 2002)

Friedman, Tom
1,000 Unforgettable Senior Moments
(Workman Publishing, 2006)

Gilman, Mary Louise
Humor in the Court
(National Court Reporters Association, 1977)

Hendrickson, Robert
British Literary Anecdotes
(Facts On File, 1990)

Holder, Judith
Grumpy Old Women
(BBC Books, 2005)

Howard, Philip
Not Dead Yet
(Times Books, 2004)

Johnston, Brian
I Say, I Say, I Say
(Methuen Publishing Ltd, 1984)

Lederer, Richard
Disorder in Court
(National Court Reporters Association, 1996)

Metcalf, Fred (Ed.)
The Penguin Dictionary of Modern Humorous Quotations
(Penguin, 2002)

Mould, R. F.
Mould's Medical Anecdotes
(Institute of Physics Publishing, 1984)

Rees, Nigel
The Cassell Dictionary of Anecdotes
(Cassell & Co, 1999)

Rees, Nigel
The Guinness Book of Humorous Anecdotes
(Guinness Publishing Ltd, 1994)

Sampson, Anthony and Sally (Ed.)
The Oxford Book of Ages
(Oxford University Press, 1988)

Wilson, Richard
I Don't Believe It!
(Michael O'Mara Books, 1996)

Youngson, Robert and Schott, Ian
Medical Blunders
(Constable & Robinson Ltd, 1996)

I am also indebted to the following newspapers and magazines:

Aberdeen Press and Journal

Associated Press

Daily Mail

The Guardian

London Evening Standard

New Scientist

Reader's Digest

Sunday Express

The Sunday Times

The Times

The Week Magazine

World Medicine Magazine

And to the following websites:

www.ag.org/Senior-Adult-Ministries

www.anecdotage.com

www.businessballs.com

www.crikey.com

www.doctorfunnywoman.com

www.dumbcrooks.com

www.esquire.com

www.findlaw.com

www.forwardedfunnies.com/senior

www.goofball.com/news

www.imdb.com

www.innocent.english.com

www.member.aol.com

www.netfunny.com

www.news.bbc.co.uk

www.oldpeoplearefunny.com

www.pmcaregivers.com .

www.power-of-attorneys.com/law

www.pruneville.com

www.scottishwebcamslive.com/law.htm

www.seniors-site.com

www.senior2senior.org

www.seniorsworldnetwork.com

www.slinkycity.com

www.suddenlysenior.com

www.swapmeetdave.com

www.time.com/time/magazine

www.toucansolutions.com

www.wikipedia.com

and finally to Ana Sampson for her invaluable contribution.